THE SUBTLE SEDUCTIONS

THE SUBTLE SEDUCTIONS
How to Be a "Good Enough" Parent

Gertrude Blanck, Ph.D.

𝒜

Jason Aronson Inc.
Northvale, New Jersey
London

10 9 8 7 6 5 4 3 2 1

Library of Congress Cataloging-in-Publication Data

Blanck, Gertrude.
  The subtle seductions.

  Includes index.
  1. Parent and child. 2. Parenting 3. Psychology—
Popular works I. Title.
BF723.P25B56   1987   155.9'24   87-14339
ISBN 0-87668-941-1

Manufactured in the United States of America.

For Peter and Tommy

Contents

Introduction

This book is about love. It's about loving your children, wanting to live life with them in a way that satisfies you, the child, the entire family. It's different from "bringing them up," which is something you do *to* them, as though they were clay to be molded, as though it's a job to be gotten over with. This book is about living *with* them, participating in their development. It's about your life as well as theirs.

To participate means that both parties play a part. You do influence your children by your participation, but it's not a one-way street. They do something to you, too. You'll never be as you were before. Under good circumstances, all parties benefit from that kind of parent–child encounter.

Much has been written and said about what to do and what not to do to ensure that children will "come out right." Much of the time the advice doesn't work. That's not always because it's wrong. It may be because it tells you *what to do*. Childrearing books are second to diet books in providing *the* answer of the moment, only to be replaced by the answer of the next moment—the one that will *really* work.

Maybe this book is just another next one. I think not. I think it is like the diet that has to be practiced over a lifetime. It will work if you're not looking for magic.

This one is not about what to do. It's about *how to live.*

Living is not only for the child. It has to be right for you and for the other children as well. Even for Grandma and Grandpa, if they're in the picture.

Since this book is about life, and life is short of perfect, it does not promise that all that will be said will be comfortable, especially in the short run. Adults can tolerate moderate discomfort because they have a sense of time. They know that today's investment pays off in the future. Some of what you read here will provide instant gratification. Some of it will reward you only later.

Life with children is not something to get done and over with. It's the prime of your life. When it's over, if you haven't lived it, you will have missed something. All you will be is older. Better to live it while the living's good. It can be very good.

Living with others involves not action, but *inter*action. You and your children (and everyone else in your life, for that matter) interact with one another. Your baby smiles at you. You feel something that makes you respond automatically. The child feels your response and reacts to that. That's interaction. It continues for the duration of your lives together, an ever spiraling action–reaction–action–reaction.

Usually, that's called a relationship.

The ingredient that makes a relationship worthwhile is love. Love comes naturally, as a result of having been loved. You cannot learn it from a book, because it's not teachable. You have to live it. If you're lucky, you've lived it from the day you were born, or before. Maybe from the day your grandparents were born and loved, so that they could love your father and mother in turn. You can keep pushing it back to Adam and Eve.

Unfortunately, it isn't always that way. One of your ancestors, if life wasn't good enough, has had to break the chain to make it better for future generations. That's a bit harder. But it can be done.

This book is for those who have had it good and also for those who want to break the chain.

What this book is not about are the gross, abusive, damaging seductions, sexual or violent. It is for those of us who feel pain and horror that these things happen. Our subject here is the "small" seductions–the kinds that take place in every home, the kinds that are performed, not by those who cannot control themselves, but by caring parents. Because love involves seduction. We *must* engage in subtle seduction in a relationship with a child. Seduction is essential to elicit the child's interest in life, in the world around him, in the people and things in that world, into wanting to live life to the fullest. Let's call those the "good" seductions. That's why it is so necessary to know how much is just right, how much is too little, how much is too much.

Why call the good kind of relating *seduction*? Why not *luring, enticing, stimulating*? Now there's a good one. *Stimulating* might be a lot more appealing because it removes any resemblance to the destructive acts.

I have chosen to call it *seduction* because I believe that comes closer to what it really is. Maybe it's hairsplitting, but to me stimulation is not mutual. It goes in one direction, from you to someone else. You are the stimulator, while the child is stimulated, acted upon.

The idea of seduction has become so loaded that sometimes we hold back even on the necessary seductions for fear that they will be too much. At other times we become overenthusiastic and go too far. How much hugging is just right? How much imposes too much of our own need for love upon the child, who cannot and should not be required to carry that burden?

Children need to be loved in order to learn to love. That's been said many times before. But it's *their* need, especially in the beginning. What comes back to us as parents comes later. It cannot be demanded. Especially can it not be demanded to make up for whatever we might be missing. The best of parents can feel cranky, needy, lonely, ill, out of sorts. Children are not there to make all that better, but the best of us sometimes ask it of them. It is a fine line, hard to draw.

The good seductions do not have to be taught. Every good parent knows how to lure a baby into communication, into social exchange. Parents are automatic seducers. They babble to a baby, talk to an older child, hold, hug, toss in the air. They do things with their children, take them places, teach them about the world.

You don't usually think about all those things you do so naturally as seduction, but isn't it? Have you seen the sad faces of children who are not encouraged to engage with another person?

This book will be about the good seductions and about those that go too far. Mostly, you will find out what you are doing right. Like Molière's *Bourgeois Gentilhomme*, you'll find out that you are speaking prose. To a baby your babbling is not prosaic. It is poetry and music and food for the soul.

But this book will not be all reassurance. It will also be about the things we do that step over the fine line. It will tell you about what you might want to alter, about a few things here and there that will make life better for your child and you, about matters that can be corrected easily merely by giving them a slight turn. In fact, many potential problems can be prevented, so you will never get to see them. It's like vaccination. How do you know that your child will get polio? You don't, but you don't take that chance.

It will tell you where your best might be a bit better. If you've gone to all the trouble to have a child, you will feel that it's worth a little more trouble for the rewards that will come.

Yes, trouble. Some of the suggestions will be inconvenient and troublesome. If they appear to be too inconvenient, they may make you downright angry. Some will go against what you think is right, against what your mother or your neighbor or another book, or a psychologist from a different school of thought, advises. You have the right to choose your advisors.

If you get angry, try to rethink it before you turn off completely. I don't mind if you get angry at me. I know that if you think it over, you may find that you were doing some things for reasons other than the good of the child. We all do. My intention is to make you aware of them.

Above all, I hope you will not feel guilty. Guilt never serves to improve a situation. People are not saints. We all have our blind spots. It's not a guilt trip to have someone help you see.

If you can accept that, a bit of inconvenience may turn out to be a rewarding trade-off. Like vaccination, it may be a momentary painful pinprick that will prevent a lot of trouble later.

This book is not for the person who values convenience above all. It is written for the "good enough" parent. "Good enough" is an idea given us by D. W. Winnicott, an English psychoanalyst. He meant to convey that there is no such thing as a perfect parent. A good enough parent can get to the end of his or her rope at times and want to give the kids back to wherever they came from. These are normal feelings. A child will thrive with a parent who is good enough.

We can put it all on a balance scale. You can make mistakes, you can be downright wrong, you can have your individual foibles. That goes on one side of the scale. On the other side are love, good intentions, interest, common sense, the ability to exercise restraint, an open mind to sound psychological knowledge, a reasonably contented life, a happy marriage if that is possible, *and* a willingness to be slightly inconvenienced at times.

For the good enough parent, the favorable side far outweighs the rest.

Children are more than an inconvenience. Often they are even hard to come by. Many people who don't conceive easily will go to a great deal of trouble to have a child. In the days when women were blamed for everything, we heard words like *barren*. A barren womb is a sad place. Now we have words like *infertility* to spread the blame to the man as well, as though it's anyone's fault.

At any rate, most of those who can, do. And many of those who cannot, continue to try, seek medical advice, adopt, inseminate, and even try new gimmicks like in vitro fertilization, surrogate gestation, and whatever will come next.

Why do most people want children? They're expensive as well as inconvenient. It costs a small fortune to feed and clothe them, educate them, provide medical care, give them some frills if you can afford it.

They're a lot of trouble, worry, grief. They curtail your freedom. They are dirty, messy, screamy. Until the baby begins to smile at you, you get nothing but crying, sometimes colic, diapers, sleepless nights, and upchuck. When you have more than one, they fight. With one you have to provide entertainment. Some become fussy eaters, poor sleepers, microorganism catchers. They get sick just when you want to go on vacation. When they grow up they leave you.

As they grow, they develop special needs. Some need eyeglasses, special shoes, orthodontia, tonsillectomies. They break bones to keep the orthopedist busy. You hope they don't have any real illnesses or handicaps, but some do, and that makes life a lot harder.

If you are middle class you also worry about the quality of the schools. If the public schools are too bad you have to make sacrifices. Private schools take a huge slice out of the budget. Working-class parents worry about the schools too, but there's not much they can do about it.

Some children need tutoring, special schools—not always because they are handicapped. Some are talented. Then you want to give them music lessons, art lessons, tennis, dancing.

You become a chauffeur, if you're not working and have the time. If you work you have to pay someone else to do the driving around. You feel uneasy about allowing a young child to use public transportation these days, assuming there is any. Many communities don't have public transportation. You're lucky if there are school buses. After school hours it's all up to you. You drive the kids to the doctor, to play with friends, to Little League, to all those lessons.

You cook for them. You may not need regular meals, but the kids do. You do the grocery shopping. When?

Your evenings are not your own. You help them with their homework, play games, read to them. At the end of the day you're exhausted. Then it's time to do the laundry. Eventually you can go to bed, but you're still on duty. You listen in your sleep for crying, coughing, breathing.

If you are two working parents, all that trouble is doubled. If you are a single parent, triple it.

This book is for parents who do it willingly (most of the time) and who want to live it in the best way possible without expecting too much of themselves. Try to remember that at your best you can only be "good enough," and that will do more than just nicely.

Why do we do it?

We do it because life isn't lived to the fullest without them.

What do we get besides inconvenienced? Life. Renewal. We fulfill a psychological urge. We do it because we are going with something we can't resist. Parenthood is the phase-appropriate role for an adult between the ages of twenty and forty whose circumstance allows it. The ideal circumstance is still a good marriage. We haven't invented anything better yet.

Not everyone can manage that. There are the misfortunes of life that leave a parent without a spouse. There are also the choices people make to be single parents.

A child is our present and our future. It's trite to repeat that children are the only immortality we can count on. Some religions say that there is an afterlife. Others are not so sure. Children are a sure thing. We hope our children will grow up and have children so that our genes will live after us. Genes are the only part of our bodies that can be perpetuated.

Children also help us grow up, to the extent that we haven't yet. We have no choice but to fulfill our adulthood when a child is in the picture. If we haven't grown up by the time they come, it is forced upon us. Without children we can indulge ourselves, be childish until we are seventy if we can get away with it. Children don't let us get away with it. A child needs an adult, so we had better become one. It's not pleasant to see a thirty year old getting into a brawl with a two year old.

We have to be adults to bring up children, but, paradoxically, we relive our childhood in the process.

If we have children, we live childhood at least twice—once in our own childhood and again with each child we have. If we are lucky we get another round with our grandchildren. Some people, if they started early enough, get still another round.

As we raise our children, we relive learning to walk and talk and play. We see the circus all over again through the child's delight. Even ice cream tastes better as we smack our lips with the child's discovery of it.

What a delight to see the wheels turning and the lights going on in children's minds as they begin to think. The why, why, why may become tedious, but it's so much fun to teach and watch as they begin to learn.

We see ourselves duplicated in our children. She has my eyes even though she has your mother's complexion and looks a little like your grandfather. He looks like you, but he has my bone structure. Psychologists call that "healthy narcissism."

Parents want their kids to do better than they did. That's why they teach them. In the novel *The Natural*, by Bernard Malamud (made into a movie starring Robert Redford), the boy's father was a minor-league ballplayer. He taught his son, who became good enough for the majors. Pablo Picasso's father was a so-so painter. He taught his son and recognized ungrudgingly that he was a genius.

We can't all produce geniuses, but most of us enjoy what we get. Your child doesn't have to have special talent. The average child will give you plenty of delight as he discovers the world. You discover all over again what you already know, but it's more fun this time around.

Those are some of the rewards. And it's not pie in the sky. It's here and now. A hug at the end of a trying day wipes away all the confusion and fatigue. "You are the best Mommy in the world" makes you glad you did it. "Daddy, you're so wonderful." You can't buy it for money.

You see your youngster becoming a strong, competent person. You hope she becomes somebody you will be proud of. More often than not that happens. You'll be able to sit back in your old age and feel fulfilled. You have memories. You'll have grandchildren if you're lucky. The cycle goes round again.

So, fortunately for posterity, most people decide that it's worth the trouble. This book is for them.

In it you will find some very profound psychological theories presented simply, through life stories. Most of the stories will be about "normal" family life that could have been made better with a few small changes. A few stories will be extreme, not at all what your family is like. I put them in for contrast, to sharpen the points I wish to get across.

The characters in these stories are not real people. They are not my own cases, because my patients' confidences are inviolate. They are composites of hundreds of life histories I have heard over the years—in supervising therapists, in leading case seminars, in teaching hundreds of psychotherapists, by listening to their case presentations in the classroom, by lecturing on three continents and learning that people's problems are the same the world over.

Despite the fictionalized characters and situations, the problems are real. You will recognize them in your friends and relatives, in the people at your workplace, in the family next door.

Chapter 1

Life after Thirty

It was nearly five o'clock on Saturday afternoon. Bill got into his car and headed for the next town. They might recognize him in his own neighborhood. He picked up a six-pack on his way to the VCR rental. It was not yet crowded. People were beginning to drift in to pick up their Saturday night videos. Bill made for the room behind the sign that said that those under eighteen could not enter.

He picked up three cassettes with his favorite actress, Ginger Lynn, pictured on the boxes. She was a blonde, nude in the first picture except for a tiny patch over her mound, stretched out on a sofa. Bill took the package off the shelf and looked around for another one starring Ginger. He found her, this time in an embrace with someone of indeterminate gender. His or her back was to the camera so that only the moderately long hair and shoulders appeared as he or she bent over Ginger. Bill found a third, this one with another woman and a man doing something vague but enticing with Ginger.

Bill had never seen these particular cassettes before, but he knew Ginger well. He had seen nearly all of her videos and would have to move on to something else soon. The excitement was wearing off. He was getting ready for a new turn-on.

Since his wife of two years walked out of their garden condo, he had haunted the porno rentals. Not that he hadn't done it before. But it was harder to manage while they were still married. He used to have to wait for her night out with her friends. Even then, he always worried that she might walk in while he was masturbating. He kept the lights out, but the TV monitor lit up the room.

They'd known each other for over a year before they married. Bill was thirty-two and Joan twenty-nine when they decided to make their relationship permanent. Their parents were delighted. They seemed just right for each other, as they say. And even though Joan's parents had tried to be very modern and casual about their living together, it was a relief to them when the wedding plans were announced.

Everyone expected that it would go well. After all, they had lived in Bill's apartment for eight months and got along well except for a few small arguments over whose job was what. Bill was a better cook but didn't like doing it every evening. They settled that easily enough. When it was Joan's turn they had takeouts from the local deli or Chinese. They took turns pushing the vacuum cleaner.

Things looked promising. Sex was great. They didn't talk to their parents about that. They just said that they got along well together. Joan's mother did ask about sex once. Joan said it was okay.

They thought it would go on forever. It took a while to realize that the certainty of marriage spoiled it. Joan still wanted sex. Oddly, Bill lost interest. He didn't realize that it was because it was real life. That made it dull.

He had kept his old *Playboys* from his bachelor days. He had to find a place to hide them, which was a nuisance. Why did they still arouse him when he had a real, live wife? When the video rentals came along, the stills in *Playboy* couldn't compete. The videos had nothing plots, but the movement more than made up for that. He wasn't into it for the story.

He went crazy over Ginger and rented every video she appeared in. Until she began to pall too.

Joan had never done some of the things Ginger did. If he'd asked her she might have tried, especially later on, when he hardly approached her at all. She was so desperate she'd have done anything. He did try a few kinks once or twice. It didn't work. Doing it didn't have the zing of watching it.

They began to fight more. Not about sex. They couldn't talk about that. They fought about almost everything else. Trivial things like her friends, whom he'd never liked, or how much money he spent on his shirts. Once or twice he slapped her. Not hard. He wasn't inclined to be brutal.

One day she announced that she was leaving. He watched tearfully as she packed and walked out. He didn't want that to happen, but he couldn't find a way to persuade her to stay. She might have been willing if he could have made love to her again as in the old days. He wanted to try, but couldn't. The pornos gripped him.

He could have begun dating again. There were women who looked good enough. He tried it. It was dull.

Jane was nearly forty and had two children when her marriage went sour. She had met Al when she was twenty-six, and that was it. She'd been working as a copywriter in a small advertising agency and didn't like it much, which meant that she would never make it big in advertising. Al was a lawyer who had just made partner in a large firm. That looked promising. He was thirty and had a Manhattan apartment and a good future. They decided to have children right away. Her career could come later.

Jane had never been crazy about sex, but she didn't exactly loathe it. She liked the cuddling and body contact. She could have lived without the rest of it but, of course, she yielded to whatever

Al wanted to do. He never did anything that could even remotely be called kinky. He was too straight for that. Besides, he could feel Jane's need to get it over with. It was lonely for him. She wanted to be able to enjoy it. She just couldn't.

Al began to have to stay late at the office. Of course, that was part of the bucking for partner, but now that he had made it, he could have eased off a bit. There was always something that could wait for the next day, but he chose to finish his work every night, no matter how late it got. He had company. The associates stayed late, hoping to make partner. Some were good-looking women. They'd all go out for a late supper together. After awhile it became Al and Elaine. One night he took her home. He phoned Jane to say that he had to stay all night proofreading a corporate document at the printer's.

He couldn't get away with that forever. He left Jane after a couple of months. He hated leaving the kids, but what could he do? He had never imagined that sex could be as super as it was with Elaine.

Eleanor's problem was different. She was nearing thirty-nine and had stopped dating. Before that, it had been a whirlwind. There were always men if you knew where to look. But she got tired of them after a while. At first she used to put herself out to listen to them. Their interests became hers.

With Joe it was trotting races. They'd spend two or three nights a week at Yonkers Raceway. He never asked whether she liked it. With another guy it was hockey. She didn't find Madison Square Garden much different. At least there was fresh air in Yonkers.

She talked it over with her friends. They had long telephone conversations, late into the night. They all agreed that men are selfish. They began to go out together in a group or two at a time. Someone suggested a women's bar. It was not hard to get picked up there. She went home with a woman thinking maybe this was for her. She was disappointed when she found she didn't like it.

She began to think she was asexual, whatever that meant. She could see the years alone looming before her.

Bob, too, was nearing forty. He thought of it as the deadline. He didn't know why he couldn't form a permanent relationship. Not that he hadn't tried. But women just didn't understand him. He talked about all the right things. Sports in moderation, unless it was tennis, which women seemed to like better than football. He also knew music. He did the museums and galleries as well as the concerts. Often, because of the right connections, he could get into the latest club, sometimes even on opening night.

But women were so demanding. He couldn't figure them. He was attractive, interesting, and—he thought—a good lover. He knew all the things that are supposed to turn women on. And they worked. Women loved it, but they left him anyway. One of them who was taking a course in psychology called him a narcissist.

It began to look as though he would have to go it alone for the most part. He did not intend to live without women. He could always have them. But it became tedious to have to go all out to make an impression on a new woman.

He had it down to a science, and he knew he was good at it. Trouble was that the same line and the same routine bored him. It became a chore. The results were so predictable. He had never met a woman who wasn't enchanted by his line. Only he was bored.

He found himself dating less and less frequently. He was afraid he would end up as one of those fussy old bachelors whose married friends would invite him to dinner now and then more out of pity than for his charming company.

Alice and John decided that they would probably stay married, mainly for the sake of the kids. It wasn't great. They had some rough times. They didn't seem able to agree on much. They were out of sync, not only about sex, although that had a lot to do with it. When he wanted it, she was tired. Rough day with the kids, you know. Maybe tomorrow night. But that made him so mad he didn't even try for another week. By then she put him off again. When he stopped trying she began to come on to him. Then he put her off.

They didn't know whether they would have extramarital affairs. They thought they might agree to it in a civilized way later on. Now things were too touchy. They had to appear like a family for the kids' sakes.

Does life have to be like that?

Chapter 2

How It Got That Way for Bill

Bill was the third of four children—two girls older than he and another boy younger. His father was a family physician in Scarsdale, a New York suburb. He did well, but not as well as the doctors in the glamorous specialties, so the family was on the poor side in that very wealthy community. By ordinary standards they were far from poor. Nobody is poor in Scarsdale. The dayworkers and gardeners come in from Mt. Vernon and New Rochelle.

Bill's father could have done better elsewhere, but the family stayed because the schools were so good. Bill's parents cared about their children; on a practical, day-to-day basis, that meant mostly his mother. His father was too busy to do the everyday things. His mother had one in help, which is not much for Scarsdale—an au pair girl from Germany, really a homesick teenager. She was needed because Bill's mother spent so much time chauffering the kids. They couldn't get to school, to music lessons, to dancing class, to Little League, without her.

When Billy was born, they were happy to have a boy after two girls. His mother was experienced with babies by then, but a boy seemed different. She was a sophisticated woman who knew in her head what to expect, but on a gut level, the boy's genitals always looked a little strange to her. She felt more comfortable handling girl babies, although she would not have been able to acknowledge this, even to herself. One would have had to observe very closely to have noticed her discomfort. No one but Billy was that close, and he was a baby so he couldn't say, but he must have sensed some vague and indefinable uneasiness, conveyed to him without words. He would not be able to define it until he hit the therapist's consultation room thirty-odd years later.

They'd decided not to have Billy circumcised. His father's partner, also a family physician, did pediatrics and obstetrics as well as general medicine. He was the family's doctor. His father was the partner's family's doctor. The partner and Billy's father agreed that circumcision is unnatural. Billy's mother was instructed to clean under his foreskin when she bathed him. She tensed up and went about it a bit too vigorously. Most doctors don't think of those things, or that an uncircumcised boy will need to have his penis handled by someone for a long time before he can clean it himself.

As Billy got older, it would have been better if his father had supervised his bath. Children get aroused, as anyone can notice if they are astute enough. They become more aroused by the parent of the opposite sex. It's unfair because they are not yet physically capable of discharging the tension.

But Billy's father had office hours at bath time. As soon as Billy was able to sit, his mother threw the three kids into the tub together. When the younger sister began to pull on Billy's penis, he howled, and their mother put a stop to it. She was a caring mother and would have stopped it without the howling.

When Billy was about ten months old, his parents took a two-week vacation. They were tired. Heaven for parents is a chance to sleep late. They made responsible arrangements. Billy's grandmother came to stay with the children. And the au pair girl was there to help her with the housework. Even though Billy had seen

Grandma before, he was at the age when everyone who isn't Mommy is a stranger. He cried a lot, but no one really knew how much his mother's absence hurt. He seemed to recover when she returned. The scars didn't show—at least not until years later. No one connected his teenage depression with mother's disappearance so many years earlier.

When Billy was three, Jonathan was born. Their mother prepared the children during her pregnancy. Billy played with his trucks while she explained things to the girls. He listened but, of course, didn't understand much—or so his mother thought. After all, he could only speak in simple sentences. She didn't realize that he could hear and absorb more than he was able to let on. He absorbed with many misunderstandings and distortions.

Their mother felt proud of her ability to tell the girls all about it without her doctor husband, who was too busy. After all, she had majored in biology in college and knew the right things to say. And she had the advantage of being able to use one of her husband's obstetrics books for illustrations. She believed in providing accurate information. She even told them what the delivery would be like.

There's a story about another mother who believed in full disclosure. Joey came home from school one day and asked his mother where he came from. "At last," she thought. She'd wondered why he hadn't asked before. She had been advised to wait until the child asks. Now she could launch into the whole story. She described conception, gestation, delivery—the works. Joey listened politely, then said, "Gee, Mom, I only wanted to know where I come from. Dick said in school today that he comes from Chicago. Where do I come from?"

Billy did get a special talk about the baby. His mother didn't think he needed to be told much—only that he would have a brother or sister, and wouldn't that be nice. He said yes, it would be nice. The yes was automatic. He was past the no stage. But how could he have known whether it would be nice or not nice? It was outside his experience.

He couldn't figure out what he needed another sister for. Two gave him a hard enough time. If it turned out to be a brother, he was told, he'd have a playmate. When he saw the baby he thought, "This thing is no fun to play with."

Billy's mother would have liked to have had one of those family deliveries where everyone is present—a family event, like Thanksgiving or Christmas or, better put, a real, live birthday party. That was out of the question because her husband's colleagues would have ostracized him for deviating from approved medical procedure.

This saved the children from the horror of having to watch a delivery. Some people think it's wonderful for children to see everything. They don't realize that it overloads their circuits. Frightened children are like lobsters being plunged into boiling water—too terrified to scream.

Nobody thought anything but good about providing biologically and medically accurate information for the children. The girls were six and eight, going to school, very verbal. It's hard to know what children understand of complex explanations with big words that they don't use every day with their friends. Only their therapists find out later what they were thinking then. By then the kids are grown and it's hard to dredge up those long-forgotten thoughts.

Forgotten but not gone. Those events from the dim past exert influence from their underground hideout, the unconscious. We don't like to think that we are influenced by factors beyond our control, so the unconscious is out of fashion. Yet everyone talks about it. Some compromise by calling it the *subconscious;* for some reason that feels better.

Of course, children need to be told something about birth. But some people go to extremes to counteract the twin evils of former times, telling too little or lying about the stork. It's a matter of what, how much, and, most important, what dosage for which age. Billy's father knew a lot about how to calculate dosages of medications for his patients, studying the individual reactions to a drug and altering the dosage accordingly. Medications for children are dosed by age and body weight. Why didn't Billy's mother know that about obstetrical information? In her eagerness to tell all, she OD'd them, the youngest most of all.

The girls, in their own ways, were as bewildered as Billy was. Each child processes information in accordance with his age level and ability to absorb. Then each forms individual fantasies to conform with his limited life experience. These fantasies, too, are largely forgotten.

No one ever found out what the girls fantasized, because they never went into therapy. Bill found out, in the course of his therapy, that unconscious fantasies direct our behavior unbeknownst to us. He could not have told you why he was absorbed by the pornos. His therapist helped him dig up the unconscious fantasies bit by bit.

Little Billy saw his mother's enlarging abdomen. He was told that the baby was in there, in Mommy's tummy. He fantasized: Could he grow a baby in his tummy? Things get into the stomach by eating. But he heard Mommy tell the girls that Daddy puts the baby into her. Where? Must be into her mouth. He heard her talk to the girls about their vaginas, but he couldn't figure out what that was. From her tone of voice, it sounded like something desirable. If that was so, he wanted one too.

Daddy stuck things into people. Billy knew that from getting his shots. His father didn't give him the shots, but in Billy's mind his father's partner was acting as his father's surrogate. Even children whose fathers are not doctors experience the doctor as acting in the parents' behalf; parents take children to the doctor and allow these things to be done to them. Billy knew that his father gave shots to other kids. Could one of the shots be for putting a baby in his tummy? He wanted one so that he could be like Mommy. Then he became afraid of it. Boys couldn't have babies, he was told. If he had one, would that make him a girl?

He'd looked at his sisters in the bathtub, of course. They had nothing there, just a slit. Is that where their penises had been? Had Daddy's partner cut them off? Why? Maybe because it feels so good when Mommy cleans it or when someone helps you urinate. They all helped him—mother, sisters, au pair girl.

Each had a distinctive touch. His mother was all business. She never got over her uneasy feeling about handling a boy, and it was continually conveyed to Billy, although never in words. Psychologists call that *unconscious communication.*

When the girls toileted Billy, they stroked his penis lovingly. The au pair girl was excessive. She had no boyfriends, and not much time off to find any. They all held Billy's penis for him when Billy could have done that for himself. All that was really necessary was to help him undo his pants. A child old enough to be toilet trained is old enough to do it himself.

The contradictory attitudes toward his penis thoroughly confused Billy. His mother handled it gingerly. His sisters, lovingly. The au pair girl, seductively. His father, reluctantly—when he was around.

Billy continued to fantasize. Maybe the girls lost theirs because it felt so good to poke it at Mom. He used to snuggle against her leg and rub it against her. He could pretend he was Daddy. Is that what Daddy did? Then how come his wasn't cut off? Maybe because he was the one who did the cutting. Mommy had told the girls there would be blood when the baby came. She did believe in telling the whole truth.

Did the girls bleed when theirs was cut off? Is having a baby like that? Mom even told them, when she thought he wasn't listening, that they would bleed when they got older. That had something to do with babies too. Obviously you have to lose your penis when you have a baby. That must be how Mommy lost hers. But how did the girls lose theirs, then? Billy went around in circles with that one.

Maybe Mommy still had a penis under her hair. Daddy did. You could see his more easily. Maybe the girls' penises would grow back and be hidden like Mommy's when they got hair there. Would he look like Mommy, or would his penis be more visible, like Daddy's, after they cut it off and it grew back? Would it grow back? His hair and fingernails always did. That didn't reassure him.

Would Daddy or his partner cut his off because he pretended to be Daddy when he rubbed against Mommy? He saw Daddy doing something more than just rubbing when they went to Disney World that time. They stayed in a large room with two big beds. The girls slept in one bed and Mommy and Daddy in the other. There was a rollaway for him. They thought he was asleep, but he heard some frightening noises. It scared him. They were moaning as though they were sick. And all that bumping around. Mommy had told the girls that Daddy put the baby into her. Was that how? Did it hurt both of them? It sounded so painful. Mommy seemed to be getting the worst of it.

He loved Mommy and wanted to be like her. She seemed to be closer to the girls. If he were a girl, would he be able to be closer to her? But he also wanted to be like Daddy; that seemed only natural for a boy. He was confused. Could he be what he wanted to be? Who controlled it all? Was it up to God, to Daddy; could he himself will it? If he could, that would be the worst. What if he made the wrong decision?

Then there was Greta, the au pair girl, who slept in his room. He had seen her naked many times. She even let him fondle her breasts. They felt so soft. Would he have breasts? She sulked around the house most of the day. Sometimes he saw her crying. Was she crying because she lost her penis?

On the nights when his parents went out, she let them all watch television, with Billy on her lap. She fondled his penis and then he didn't miss Mommy so much. This was the standard way of soothing children where she came from. No one thought of it as child abuse; they never even heard of fancy ideas like that. It soothed him and relieved her homesickness at the same time.

So Billy had a retinue of penis handlers: the doctor, when he examined him; his father, who helped him urinate, and whose image was merged with that of the doctor-partner; his mother, when she bathed him and helped him with his toileting; his sisters; the au pair girl. Yet he was scolded when he handled himself. They told him never to do that. Was it theirs or his? He wasn't sure.

Mommy went to the hospital when her tummy got very big. She let him feel it before she went. She told him that his brother or sister was doing all that moving inside, and that it was getting to be time for her to go to the hospital to get the baby out. How would they get it? They'd have to cut her open.

After the baby came, Daddy took them all to the hospital to see Mommy and Jonathan. He was glad to see Mommy again, but a little scared of the hospital. The baby didn't look like much.

Billy missed Mommy while she was away. He was reminded, vaguely, of how bad he had felt when they went away on vacation. He couldn't remember the event; only the feelings remained. But Greta took him into bed with her when he cried. He liked the way she smelled. No one thought anything of that, either. After all, it comforted him. She got used to taking him into her bed after that. The comforting was mutual. He was a live teddy bear.

Mommy was tired when she came home from the hospital. They hired a woman to take care of the baby at first. Billy didn't like having the baby in the house. He began to comfort himself with the idea that Jonathan was the woman's baby. Maybe the woman had brought Jonathan here so that he could suck on Mommy's breasts. When she left, though, she forgot to take her baby with her. The baby slept in Mommy's and Daddy's room. Why couldn't he?

Life settled down. Billy gradually realized that nothing was going to be all that different for him. He went to nursery school, kindergarten, elementary school. He had a love-hate relationship with Jonathan as they both grew. Sometimes he was fun to play with. Most of the time he got too much of everything. Billy learned elementary math and physics early. He learned to count and to measure with his eyes. Was Jonathan getting more cookies, a fuller glass of shake, a longer hot dog? Would Jonathan's penis get to be bigger than his? Was Jonathan's glass bigger, or was there more in it?

Bill did well at school and was popular with the other kids at Scarsdale High. He seemed like the typical, privileged teenager. He tried a little pot, a little sex. He didn't go for the hard drugs. He had a bright future. From Scarsdale High one could get into the Ivy Leagues.

No one thought he had problems. Adolescent moods, yes. But he would outgrow them. He seemed a little low-keyed, that's all. His father talked to him about sex, unaware that he had already tried it. He was lucky enough not to have had to use the backseat of the car. The girl invited him to her house while her parents were on vacation in Bermuda. The housekeeper was in her own room and didn't care much anyway. The girl had experience and took his penis into her hand to guide it in. It went flat in her hand. That was a double downer.

He wasn't as much trouble at home as some of his friends were. He was helpful around the house and didn't raise many storms. His parents felt lucky. Who wants teenage storms? They had enough with the girls. What they didn't notice was that he was too good, and too sad, most of the time. He masturbated a lot, but he was able to conceal that. It didn't worry him. He knew that all teenagers do that. But he became wary of girls. He didn't want any more failures.

Things picked up a bit in college. The girls were older. Some were bitchy, but some were kind. He found a girl who had a mission. She helped him a lot. She would talk to him and make up stories while they made love. She had a good imagination and could change the stories when they no longer excited him. He always got aroused when she introduced a new twist to the story.

He began to gain confidence in his prowess. He tried other women, with varying success. He learned how to tell himself stories. And a little pot always helped.

After college he got a good job as an electronics engineer. He got an apartment in the city. There were lots of women. Lovemaking became an uncertain chore. He did better with the centerfold of *Playboy*.

Then he met Joan. He only failed the first time with her. They began to make up stories during lovemaking. That did it. They played them out. They didn't think of the stories as kinky—just play acting.

His favorite was to be stranded on a desert island with Joan, the only two survivors of a plane crash. Rescue is slow. She is married and is determined not to be unfaithful no matter how long the rescue takes. He pleads and pleads. He forces himself upon her, not too violently. She yields.

They decided to move in together. They got along fairly well. Sex was better than he had ever dreamed it could be. The next step was marriage. They had both grown up in the suburbs and didn't like the pace of the city. They found a great condo on Long Island, with tennis courts and all. They thought about children.

After about eight months it began to tax their imaginations to keep on creating new twists to the stories as the old ones wore out. The plots became rougher, and they always ended with forcing. Without realizing it, he became rough with her. She began to object. She called him a pervert for needing all that. He tried it without the stories. He couldn't get an erection. They fought. She called him some choice names, said he wasn't much of a man. Maybe he was gay. He didn't think so. Then the videotapes came out. There were his stories, ready-made.

It got to the point where they couldn't patch it up anymore. They agreed to separate. The videos absorbed him. He thought all day about what he would rent that night. His work began to suffer.

Chapter 3

One Incident Doth Not a Neurosis Make

The insidious thing about the subtle seductions is that their consequences are not immediately discernable. Like small doses of arsenic, the effects are cumulative.

In Bill's case, not much showed until he was a teenager. Even then, no one noticed because his symptoms were so convenient. He was mildly depressed and too compliant for his own good. It was good for everyone else. His parents and teachers did not notice that he was depressed. They thought of him as serious minded, a much valued trait in their opinions. And who would complain about compliance?

For some teenagers, the accumulated toxins become tragic. The child contains them for fifteen years or so. Then it all bursts out into something terrible. A quiet kid goes berserk, commits murder. The inquiring reporter interviews the neighbors. He was always so good, so polite. Big headlines, "Why, why, why?"

Bill's tragedy took longer to build, and it never hit the newscasts. He did not have any *acute* emotional trauma in his childhood. Nothing that anyone could point to. No serious illnesses or accidents, no deaths in the immediate family, no divorce, no violence, not even much parental quarreling. He lived a better-than-average life in a better-than-average nuclear family that had better-than-average material advantages.

Bill's parents were pleased with the way he turned out, until his divorce. That baffled them. Then they wondered what they had done wrong.

Parental guilt is a twentieth-century disease. The Edwardians upheld the tradition of blaming the little rascals for not behaving like little adults. Then came Freud, who turned psychology on its ear, mostly for the better, except for guilt.

Ever since Freud discovered that childhood experiences exert a powerful influence upon the adult outcome, parents have claimed all the credit, good and bad. That is hardly what Freud meant, but it has been understood that way.

There's the joke about the mother bragging to the neighbors about her successful son. He has a good job, a Porsche, a Manhattan apartment, and a psychoanalyst. "And what does he talk about to his psychoanalyst? Me."

Another child in Bill's circumstance would have turned out differently. Maybe better, maybe worse. Not that babies can do anything to change the world they are born into. Human infants are the most helpless of all newborn animals. They have to make the best of what they get. By and large, however, our native abilities have much to do with what we make of life. That should relieve parental guilt, but it probably won't. Parents are too fond of guilt to give it up without a struggle.

So unless babies' small worlds are exceedingly damaging, they make do. If they are born into a world of mental illness, violence, alcoholism, or drug addiction, even the best copers are licked before they start.

Life is hard for babies and young children, even under ideal conditions. The saying goes that being a child is hard, until you grow up; then being childish seems easier.

There is so much that children have to try to understand, with such limited experience to go on. But they don't come into the world entirely naked, psychologically speaking. They have their built-in assets, including the ability to create fantasies, an indispensable coping device. Children use it to make sense of experiences that would otherwise be too bewildering and frightening. That doesn't mean that the fantasies they create would make sense to an adult. They are, after all, products of inexperienced minds.

Fantasies are tapestries. Children use each thread of experience, add threads from their imaginations, and weave them into unique designs. Some are artistic, some ordinary. It depends upon a combination of the child's talent and the material— experiences—he has to work with.

At its least, fantasy is utilitarian, and life would be empty and dull without it. It is that way for those with limited ability to create fantasies. Such people need lots of stimulation from outside themselves because of emptiness inside. They are addicted to noise, excitement, crowds, blaring radios, television all day and night, drugs for "recreation."

Those of us who are ordinary use fantasy to enrich our inner lives and keep us company. Novels, theater, movies, television give fresh color to our tapestries when they begin to fade. The geniuses among us don't need so much continuous addition of new color from the outside. They have an abundance within. They create fantasy material for the rest of us by converting their own fantasies into art, music, poetry.

So it is not at all unusual that Billy had fantasies. It would have been strange if he hadn't. And he put them to the best possible use—to try to make sense out of all that was puzzling to him. But there was too much, too many threads to keep track of. A boy with less fantasy-creating skill would have become even more troubled. His threads would have tangled. That's when symptoms such as tantrums, tics, learning disabilities, and sleep disorders begin to show, and people take notice.

That is not to say that Billy was not troubled, only that he contained it. Children like Billy slip by the guidance counselors.

Let us look at how the threads of Billy's tapestry multiplied, how the real events in his life were interwoven with his imagination into a fabric that was barely visible in his childhood, but later enveloped his life.

His mother was not comfortable with handling a boy, even though she was consciously pleased to have one. Billy could not have known this as a baby; his mother didn't even know it. But the feeling seeped in and established the first invisible thread: uncertainty. This is not one of those strange ideas that psychologists propose every now and then in order to earn their keep. Sensitive mothers and baby nurses have always known that babies "feel" the caregiver's feelings.

It might not have amounted to much in and of itself, because Bill had such good endowments, such as strong inborn masculinity. That can vary from child to child. Bill had it in good measure. Another was his vivid imagination and ability to use fantasy. Nevertheless, confusion about himself and his body was destined to grow as more and more was added to that first thread.

The next thread: Every child, at about the age of a year and a half, becomes aware of sex difference. It is always a shock to the child to notice that not everyone is the same. Especially shocking is the discovery, with the limited perception of childhood, that there are haves and have nots, for so it appears. Children at that age want everything everyone else has — toys, cookies, body parts. A girl wants what the boy has, and it is no consolation to her to be told that she has something too. Where is it? Inside. Ha!

Nor are boys consoled to be the possessors. The visible fact that girls don't have it proves that what one possesses at one moment can be taken away at the next. It happens with their toys all the time, especially if they have siblings.

That shock can be taken in stride if it is not reinforced. Billy had plenty of reinforcement. He had daily exposure to his sisters in the bathtub, without time in between for shock absorption. He was also exposed to adult nudity.

Many people believe that that's the "natural" way to live. *Natural* has become synonymous with *good*. Look at food packaging.

So many foods are now labeled "natural" that one would think that all the other stuff is unnatural. Commercials bombard us about the virtues of "natural fiber." It wouldn't be worth a chemist's time to create synthetic fiber. Mushrooms are natural. Some varieties are detrimental to your health.

Despite the argument of the naturalists, children are blown over by the disparity between a child's and an adult's body. Young children do not have an adult's sense of time. You can tell them that they will grow up to be that way some day. (If you do, be sure you're talking about the parent of the same sex.) What gets across to them is another matter.

When he compared his body with his father's, little Billy could feel only inferiority and jealousy. It undermined his self-esteem. The daily exposure to his mother's nudity reinforced Billy's confusion. At a young age, it's normal for a boy to vacillate between wanting to be like his mother and wanting to be like his father. Usually, he comes to rest in favor of being like the parent of the same sex. Some "decide" the other way. Billy remained never quite sure.

There was no rest for Billy. He staggered from one subtle seduction to the next.

Exposure to all the varied nude bodies was a continual reminder that he was different from *everyone*. His sisters resembled one another. Greta resembled his mother. His father's body was godlike. There was nobody in the family like Billy for three years, until Jonathan arrived. Then Billy could feel somewhat superior. It always helps for there to be an underdog, unless you are it.

Poor self-esteem is one of the multiple threads that work into depression. Another is the related matter of being abandoned. When babies are left without their parents, even for a few days or weeks, the bad feelings make them feel like bad persons. Being left for a few hours, however, is good for babies. It helps them learn how to live alone.

Being left for too long at too early an age, even with the

world's best grandma, injures self-esteem in still another way.
Young children think their parents are always right. It isn't until
adolescence that they think their parents are always wrong. So
the abandoned one-year-old thinks: "I must be bad or they
wouldn't have left me. I must deserve all this painful longing for
Mommy." If parents knew how much pain it causes, they would
decide that the two weeks in Bermuda aren't worth it.

It's easy to say "Take the children with you." Even if you enjoy their company and want to take them, the hotels won't let you
do it right. What would have happened if Billy's parents had tried
to reserve a separate room for him, and still another room for the
girls, when they went to Disney World? The travel agent would
have thought they were crazy, and the hotel would have charged
enough to buy an ashtray for a fighter plane.

It was not *simply* being left for too long too soon, nor *simply*
comparison with all those bodies. It takes a fair number of
downers like that to supply threads that color the tapestry gray.

For Bill, those threads hung loose until adolescence. Then
they found company. They became interwoven with the inevitable disappointments that almost everyone experiences – failure
to make the basketball team, rejection by girls. Black threads join
the gray left over from childhood. The design acquires a somber
coloration.

We call that *depression*. Don't let anyone tell you that it's all
caused by brain chemistry and that if you jog fifteen miles a day,
you'll feel better. You'll have sore feet and feel worse.

This makes a case for avoiding the avoidable, even at some ex-
pense and inconvenience. We never know what unavoidables may
come along in the future to add more black to the tapestry. What
if Billy had needed an appendectomy later on, or had had an accident or a serious illness? What if there had been a death in the
family? Since fantasies need more than one thread for a design,
why supply dismal ones if you can help it? Life usually has a supply of those waiting.

We begin to see the accumulation of fact and fantasy in Billy's life, some normal, some inevitable, some preventable.

Injections are the lesser evil than the diseases they prevent, but you can't make a child like them. And they reinforce a tendency to passivity, if it exists for other reasons. Billy did not surrender to passivity, but he didn't conquer it either. He had to keep fighting it off. He fought it off in adult life by needing to force his partner. She had to be the one to surrender to him. Many people play at that once in a while, and it can be fun. It's not much fun if it is an essential condition of functioning. When his partner tired of it, Bill's penis lay down on the job.

Let's add it up. Our first item is the uncertainty about his body that Billy absorbed from his mother, including the overzealous and painful handling of his penis.

Now add the exposure to nudity in all its varied forms.

Then add the barrage of information about conception, pregnancy, delivery, menstruation. Billy's mother operated like the teacher in a one-room schoolhouse, teaching all ages and all grades at once. He did not need to hear what his sisters were told. (It's not certain that *they* needed all that information at once either.) It made Billy unsure about whether the same things would happen to him. Remember, his mother made it sound so desirable. He didn't want to miss out.

Part of a boy's normal wish to be like his mother is because he thinks he will be closer to her that way. Billy thought his sisters had the advantage there. But why did they have to bleed?

Now add Billy's feelings of inferiority about his body, combined with his having been left, combined with his conflicting ideas about girls and women. At times, they seemed to have intriguing advantages. Billy wanted everything – breasts, a vagina (whatever that is), a baby, closeness with mother. He had to fight those wishes because he also wanted to be a boy. Psychoanalysts call that *conflict*.

Here one might ask, "But what about his father as a masculine role model? Wouldn't that counteract the feminine wishes?" To some extent, yes. But people tend to exaggerate the influence of models and to underestimate the inner life of the child. We do not become what we see around us. We use what is around us as one of many threads. More of them come from within than from role models.

One way Billy had to counteract the wish to be like the girls was to regard them as inferior. That method is used by many, such as taxi drivers who go berserk with women drivers. Men like that are not really pigs. What they are really up to is continuously fighting for their masculinity because they never feel sure of it. There's nothing like putting a woman down to make you feel like a man!

Billy also confused femininity with passivity. He combined what he saw of his parents having intercourse with his experiences of being forced and subjugated—having his shots, going to the dentist, even having his hair cut; once or twice he'd had to have an enema.

Add everyone's involvement with his body as though his penis were a family toy. Add the homesick au pair girl. Isolated from her home, her mother tongue, her family, she turned Billy into her live teddy bear or security blanket. She overfondled him. So did his sisters. No time for him to sort out which body parts belonged to him.

Greta took Billy into her bed. Underprivileged children, more often than not, do not have their own beds. In that unfortunate situation, the necessities of life take precedence over a separate bed. Billy had his own bed. It would have taken just a bit more parental supervision to have kept him in it.

Children do get lonely in their own beds. It's more comforting to snuggle in with someone. In January in a cold climate, it's an almost irresistible temptation. Resist it. If life is satisfactory on a day-to-day basis, the brief moment of loneliness before falling asleep is good for children. It helps them find the boundaries of their own bodies, so they get to know where they end and the other person begins. They learn, too, how to soothe themselves, instead of always needing someone else. The ability to self soothe comes in handy later in life. Those who acquire it do not need alcohol or drugs whenever life takes a downturn.

A little snuggling in a rocking chair before bedtime is wonderful. Togetherness in bed is for adults with their sex partners. Many adult sex problems arise because a developmental step has been skipped. The person who has such difficulties may not have had the opportunity to find out where he or she begins and ends. The sexual encounter gets all mixed up with that priority. We have to be secure about who we are before we can take risks. Letting go in orgasm involves forgetting one's boundaries for the moment. Some people are afraid to forget. They may not remember again. Not for no reason do the French refer to orgasm as *la petite mort*, the little death.

The first symptom Billy had that might have been noticed by someone was adolescent depression. The normal adolescent rebellion, so troublesome and so dreaded by parents, was absent. He was too good, too compliant, too quiet.

It is understandable that parents would welcome this. Only a skilled psychological observer would think that he was troubled by approaching adulthood, by the awful question of whether he would be able to make it as a man. And who would think that the way he was in adolescence had its origins way back in infancy?

His uncertainty about himself, his body, his masculinity, his self-esteem was reflected in his sex problem—occasional impotence and perpetual fear of it. It is not something a young man tells friends, relatives, and investigative reporters. Bill dealt with it by using the problem-solving tool that had helped him all his life—fantasies. Now they became the stories he needed as props. That served him for a while.

But that sort of thing doesn't serve adulthood very efficiently. After a while boosters become necessary. Change the story. Use visual props, like *Playboy*. Or X-rated movies. With VCR's one is saved from the embarrassment of being seen at a porno movie, the humiliation of having to masturbate in the theatre.

In the end, Bill's fantasy life won out over real life. What served him so well in childhood destroyed his adulthood. He was suffocating in the tapestry of fantasies that wrapped itself around him.

Chapter 4

An Ordinary Woman

Jane was the younger of two. Her sister was four years older. Their parents were harried by the time Jane was born. They didn't exactly not want her. Their religion taught them to take life as it comes, especially children. Life was not easy for them. They had married young and were not prepared for what responsible adulthood demanded. When Jane's mother became pregnant, they thought maybe it was all for the best. That was short of overjoyed.

Jane's sister, Liz, had not been an easy baby. She was colicky and a poor sleeper in her first year. Her terrible twos were more terrible than most. Now her parents were looking forward to her starting school. Her mother would have a few hours' respite each day. That's when she became pregnant with Jane.

They thought they had been careful, but something slipped. They decided to let it be. As it turned out, Jane was an easy baby. Maybe too easy. Jane's mother wasn't enjoying life. Her father thought he was, at times. At other times, he didn't kid himself. He was a sales representative for a large drug company. The commissions weren't great. There was a lot of traveling, which he enjoyed at first. After a while, every hotel room looked liked every other. It got so he didn't know Chicago from Cleveland. And the nights were lonely.

Traveling wasn't good for the marriage, which hadn't been good for a long time anyway. When evenings on the road got dull, Jane's Dad took to picking up women at the bars. It didn't take much for Jane's mother to guess. She'd phone his room at night and wonder why he wasn't very talkative. When he'd come home they'd fight over it. Nevertheless, when she became pregnant they thought that might make things better.

They had hoped for a boy. Jane's mother thought her husband would be more interested in family life if they had a boy. She didn't realize that his disinterest had to do with her. She had become mildly depressed after Liz was born and couldn't pull out of it. She couldn't get interested in anything and was no fun to be with. She let her appearance go. She was no longer the vivacious girl he had known in high school.

They bowed to God's will, tried to accept another girl in good grace. They put the disappointment out of their minds, put on such a good face that not even their closest friends could tell. It all got covered over with rationalizations. Liz would have a playmate. Jane could wear the clothes that Liz had outgrown. They could share a room. It's easier to bring up girls.

For a while, it worked. The marriage did improve somewhat. Jane's father helped with the children when he was home. He made a real effort. He talked to their minister, who was supportive. But the romance that led them to marriage never returned after their children were born. They weren't up to so much work, so much responsibility, so much sharing of each other with babies, so little money, so little pleasure.

Jane's mother did her duty. Not much more. She couldn't work up any enthusiasm. She didn't realize that she was more depressed than ever after Jane was born. It just seemed that life was drab. Jane was fed and bathed and changed and taken to the pediatrician. She wasn't talked to or played with. Her mother never felt like it.

Liz pretended to play mother for a short while. She squeezed Jane too hard at times, dropped her once. Dolls were better. Liz had never had an abundance of lively interest from either parent. She didn't want to share the little there was with the baby.

Being a good baby didn't get Jane much. But had she been troublesome, it might have been worse. Her mother was not deliberately emotionally unavailable. She just didn't have it.

During her waking time Jane cooed quietly by herself. Her mother watched the soaps a lot, whether Jane was awake or not. Jane was a reaching-out baby. Some babies are, which is a good thing, because they can sometimes induce an indifferent mother to respond more actively and even to like it. Jane's mother couldn't be brought out of the dumps.

When Jane started to crawl around, she was into everything. Smart kids are curious. It became even worse when she started to walk, because her mother couldn't get up the energy to follow her around. She didn't want Jane to get hurt. She wasn't that sick. So she strapped Jane into her high chair and stroller a lot. A baby can't explore much of the world that way. It put a wet blanket on Jane's curiosity for life.

A second baby didn't mend the marriage. Babies never do. A lot of people expect it of them, but that's not what babies are for.

Jane's father started staying out evenings even when he didn't have to be out of town. Jane's mother started drinking evenings. Alcohol is not a cure for depression. And the morning hangover didn't make her a better mother.

Jane limped through early childhood on her talents. After infancy, when she cooed to herself but heard no echo, she continued to talk to herself. Not aloud. She wasn't crazy, just turned inward. She became her own best friend.

The reaching-out talent led her into bed with whomever

would have her. Liz would kick her out. Her mother was indifferent, but let her stay. Jane gathered as much warmth as she could that way—from her father too, when he was there.

Jane's looks were her salvation and could have been her downfall. Everyone outside the family liked to hug her—neighbors, the manager of the supermarket. Fortunately, she never met up with a pedophile. She let everyone hug her without squirming because it fed her famine. As she got to be five and six, it coincided with her Dad's famine. He was overwhelmed by her beauty. She outshone Liz. In his own loneliness, he held her a bit too tight, snuggled with her a bit too long. He couldn't help it and hardly knew he was doing it. That was all there was at home for him.

Jane knew very early that she had more going for her than Mom or Liz. She was prettier, smarter, more likable. It seemed natural that Dad felt more affection for her. She created a fantasy that she was not their child. They adopted her as a baby. Her real parents were rich and traveled a lot. Someday they would come for her.

The thought that her Dad was not her Dad led to more elaborate fantasies. She knew that he was getting his sex elsewhere. When she grew up he would want to marry her. Why not? They weren't related, and he liked her best. She thought about what a good wife she would make. She'd be cheerful when he came home, not down in the dumps like Mother. She'd have a good dinner ready, dress up to look her best, make life festive for him.

Jane's mother didn't talk to the girls much about sex. She did her duty, prepared them for menstruation, left out the reason for it. They found out from their friends, of course. Although she didn't mention sex, their mother made it clear by her silence that it was unmentionable, unpleasant, undesirable, something men wanted that women have to give in to. Why? The question wasn't asked.

Jane had her own answers because she felt certain stirrings. She added to the original fantasy. Now her *real* father would come for her and bring with him a gorgeous young man, someone mysterious, like Clint Eastwood, on a pale horse. Unlike the movie in which he gently lets down the young girl who falls in love with him, he goes for Jane.

The girls at school told her what she could do about her sexual stirrings. She had to; she couldn't hold off. But masturbation made her feel so guilty that it didn't seem worth it, until the next time, when the feelings became urgent again.

Masturbation saves children from erotic overload. But it is accompanied by fantasies. It's the fantasies that make them feel guilty. Jane's fantasy about Clint Eastwood barely disguised her feelings toward her father. She was accumulating guilt by the carload, even though she hardly every did anything really wrong. The worst she ever did was fight with Liz. They fought a lot, and were punished a lot. She thought she was being punished for fighting. She provoked Liz because she needed the punishment to relieve some of her guilt. It never took care of all of it.

Her parents were drifting toward the inevitable. Dad left. At first he was not in a hurry to do anything legal. Lawyers are expensive. The girls went to visit him at his apartment whenever he was in town. Because of her looks, Jane got much more affection than Liz. It didn't foster sisterly love.

When Liz was old enough to hang out with her own friends, Jane went to visit Dad alone. It was not in his mind to molest her. He wasn't that way. But he was so needy. He held her in his lap and cried about his troubles and told her how cold her mother had been to him. Jane didn't need to be told that. Her mother was cold to her, too. But he also told her how warm the other women were. Jane was rocked by that. She wanted to be what the other women were to him so that he wouldn't need them.

Those fantasies had begun long before her parents separated. Separation merely reinforced them and lent them credulity. With her mother out of the picture, Jane might be in. Strong stuff for a little girl.

It was a crusher when Dad arranged for a real divorce instead of the informal separation that led Jane to hope her parents might get together again. Kids want an intact home, their fantasies to the contrary. Fantasies are only safe if they don't come true.

Dad had been going with Judith for a year and wanted to marry her. The girls met her when they went to visit him on Sundays. They all went out to dinner. Judith made a real effort to be nice to them. Jane knew that she had lost out.

Dad wanted the girls to attend the wedding. Mother begged, pleaded, wept, and got drunk asking them not to go. She wanted a boycott. Jane was torn. She had her own reasons for not being happy about the wedding. But she didn't enjoy being manipulated by Mother. She vacillated. When she was with Mother, she wanted to end the badgering, so she agreed not to go to the wedding. When she was with Dad, she couldn't say no to him.

What decided the issue was his offer to buy her a stunning outfit—any dress she wanted, with shoes to match. She wasn't used to getting clothes, certainly not party clothes that all go together. Ordinarily there was not enough money for that. It didn't mean that Jane could be bought. Not really. Only that she was a teenager whose heart longed for something pretty to wear.

She went to the wedding with Liz. She cried every day of the honeymoon. When Dad and Judith returned, they tried to have the girls with them often. They had a spare room fixed up for them. Jane never felt comfortable there. Her fantasies were unconscious by this time, so she didn't know that she really wanted to be in Dad's room.

Jane was fourteen when Liz went off to college. Although they had never been close, Jane missed her—not for herself, but because Jane now had Mother alone, without Liz to share the burden. Mother hadn't gotten better with Dad's marriage to Judith. She drank more, neglected the house, lived life through the soaps. Jane took care of herself, went to school, did her homework, cooked something or other for both of them, found herself worrying about her mother's health. There wasn't a lot of money, and Jane took any job she could get, baby-sitting and such. It kept her away from home more and worrying about Mom more.

Jane couldn't bring herself to go away to college. She went to the local community college. She reasoned that it was less expensive, but the real reason was that she was afraid to leave mother alone. So she attended college part time and worked as a full-time typist in an advertising agency. Someone at the agency thought she had a knack for copywriting and urged her to try it. She made it, but her heart wasn't in a career. Maybe it was her mind rather than her heart. Half the time she worried about Mother; the other half was occupied with fantasies of which she wasn't even aware.

She was better off being unaware of some of those fantasies. That's one of the advantages of unconscious fantasies. They can drive you crazy if they become conscious, except under the auspices of a good psychotherapist who knows how to elicit them gradually, in tolerable doses. In Jane's childhood, adolescence, and young adulthood, it would have been more than she would have been able to bear to have known why she was so worried about her mother.

There was plenty to worry about. Mother was depressed, neglected herself, drank too much. Anyone would agree that a good daughter would worry. Only her therapist, much later in Jane's life, helped her realize that from childhood on, Jane, unbeknownst even to herself, thought it would have been better if Mother were dead.

It's natural for a child to have death wishes. Children don't know what death is. Who does know, really? Homo sapiens is the only species in which the individual knows that he or she is going to die. Most of us live life now, without keeping that dismal thought in the forefront of our minds. If we are religious, we think we will be going to a better place some day. We are not in a hurry to get there.

"I'll be the sheriff and shoot you dead. Lie down." Bang, bang. "Now get up. You can have a turn being the sheriff." Or, "I don't like you. I wish you were dead." "Now I need you, so come back."

Jane wished her mother dead more than a normal amount. She had good reason. Mother was unkind in her indifference. She didn't do anything overtly cruel, but her absence of interest didn't contribute to Jane's self-esteem. She wanted a better mother who would make her feel like a good, lovable person. "Maybe Dad would do that if I could get him to myself. So who needs Mother. If she (and Liz) were dead, there'd be just Dad and me."

That was before Judith came on the scene to kill all chances. Then Judith had to be added to the hit list. That gave Jane another carload of unconscious guilt. Her low self-esteem dropped closer to zero. One good thing, though. She never gave up on herself.

Jane met Al at an office party. He liked her looks. By this time Jane knew that her looks were her asset, and she played them up. She was not short on brains, either, but she was very short on curiosity and ambition. That suited Al. He had his own ambition, and having a wife at home would help him further his career without the bother of all the details of daily living. Without the bother for *him*, that is. Jane was glad to be able to leave the ad agency to do the housekeeping for him.

Sex wasn't new to her. She had always been attractive to boys, and a few of them in high school and college had talked her into it. She didn't get turned on. That didn't matter to the boys. They got it.

It was the same with Al. Not anathema. She was used to a bedmate for cuddling. But it was not what some people said about sex. Jane's frigidity was all right with Al for a while because the marriage served him so well in other ways. Inevitably, though, he began to want more responsiveness.

It looked to their friends, especially to the women, as though Al was selfish. He did appear to be using Jane. What didn't meet the eye was that she was unconsciously using him, too. People don't mean to use each other that way. Marriage is not like a one-time transaction where you can put something over on someone and never see them again. Some people go into marriage knowing that it's a con job, for money or some such reason. But even they can't stand it forever. That's why we hear once in a while about someone murdering a wealthy spouse. It's for the money, of course. But to a much greater extent it's because of the tedium.

Jane's marriage began to fall apart because of tedium. Al got restless because she wasn't curious, lively, interesting, sexy. Neither of them knew that Jane was unconsciously pushing him away, making herself less attractive, less interesting. They would have been surprised if someone had told them that. Jane had always thought that she would never be like her mother. She didn't want to be. But slowly, day by day, her life became a replica of her mother's. She became dull. Al left. It was a repeat.

Chapter 5

What Made Jane Tick

Jane was underseduced before she was overseduced. She was, of course, captivated by the overseduction. Wouldn't we all be? But it got to be too much. Yes, there is such a thing as too much pleasure, especially when it comes after famine. You wouldn't give a starving person a banana split with whipped cream and nuts.

The overseduction by her father came relatively late in Jane's life, if you can think of age four as late in life. It actually is the old age of early childhood. Development is so accelerated before that age that never again do we learn so much so quickly. By the age of four, our minds and hearts are ready for sex. The trouble is that our bodies are not.

The good father treads a fine line. He must convey, not in so many words, that his young daughter is attractive, so that she will develop self-esteem and expect young men to like her when the time is right. At the same time, the father has to make it very clear that he is taken, that they are a generation apart. He should not allow the slightest notion that he is sexually available to her.

Not easy to cut it so fine. One step over the line in either direction and you fall into a deep hole.

The overseduction would have been too much for a child who had had more affection in infancy. That's because humans are not biologically ready for sex until puberty. Jane was not sexually assaulted; she was just overstimulated, which teases mercilessly. This does not argue for consummation, which is far worse. There, the adult gets the pleasure (if something so sick can be called pleasure), while the child gets the pain.

Overseduction is always to fulfill the adult's need. For Jane, it was doubly unfair, because her psychological stomach lacked the digestive juices for such a rich diet. Strange as it seems, that made the underseduction attractive, not only then and there, but for life.

We all know people who avoid pleasure. Many of them rationalize it with a religious motive. Suffering will be rewarded in Heaven. Some religions prohibit dancing, music, alcohol — things that even Jane would be able to enjoy. The Shakers prohibited sex. Where are they now?

A psychiatrist would label Jane a *masochist*. Psychiatrists do not list the ingredients in their diagnoses, so the label doesn't tell us much. It doesn't even distinguish between extreme, moderate, or mild, as we would expect on a package of curry.

There's more to it than that, but we can use those three degrees of masochism for starters. Most of us would be labelled mild mashochists. Those of us who work, anyway. If we are lucky, our work is pleasurable. But even so, in order to be able to work effectively we have to be able to postpone pleasure. We look out of our office windows on a beautiful spring day and wish we could be in the country, but we don't leap out of the office and go. People who have to have it right away do not function well in this complex society of ours. So a mild masochist is a fit. A hedonist is a misfit. An impulse-ridden hedonist is a serious problem.

Jane was a moderate masochist. She reached out for some of

the good things in life. Her try at a career was less than half-hearted, but she dated, married, had children. The trouble was she couldn't stand enjoying it. As for sex, childhood masturbation was the last time she let herself enjoy that. Not that she could have reversed that simply by talking herself into allowing pleasure, or by having a sex therapist grant her permission.

Sex therapists have become popular because they know some tricks (no pun intended) for making sex pleasurable. I call them *popular mechanics*. They have devices and gimmicks—the vibrators and oils and stuff. They even have a mechanical method for delaying premature ejaculation.

The gimmicks do work for some people who are satisfied with mechanical solutions. They don't work for everyone. Chalk that up to exaggerated advertising. We know that new, extra-strength Soapo won't get your clothes any whiter than old, reliable Soapo. Sex therapy can "cure" certain mild cases of frigidity and impotence by mechanical means. The hard cases can only be cured the hard way—by psychoanalytic methods.

Jane was a hard case, a case of feast after famine that entrenched her devotion to famine. Popular mechanics cannot change that. In the battle of unconscious guilt versus vibrator, guilt always wins.

There are additional reasons for Jane's need for famine. The underseduction theme entered Jane's life first. A baby must be lured into the world of other people, must learn to relate. Good parents teach this automatically, by virtue of their own social propensities, learned when they were babies. I am calling that *non-sexual seduction*. If you don't like the term *seduction*, call it something else—luring, enticing, leading, encouraging, stimulating, interacting, enlivening, quickening. *Seduction* is more accurate, and can be accepted by grasping the idea that there are entirely proper and appropriate forms of it. We saw that a father has to seduce his young daughter just a smidgen, at the right time in her life. The same holds true for mother and son.

Babbling to a baby is one of the earliest forms of appropriate and necessary seduction. Jane wasn't babbled to when she needed it. Later, she was made to feel too attractive for comfort. Not only is there a right time for everything but, as we saw with Bill, proper dosage is important. So the nonsense that bursts from our lips whenever we see a baby is not as silly as it sounds. It seduces the baby into conversation—if you don't mind calling the give and take of babble a conversation. We become socialized that way.

Baby Jane was starved for conversation. Her mother wasn't up to it. Her father wasn't home enough. He didn't want another girl anyway. Not at first. Not until he needed her for his own purposes later on. So nobody babbled much with Jane.

A baby less favorably endowed than Jane might simply have given up. At best, such babies withdraw into themselves, grow up strange, isolated, living in a world of their own. With extreme emotional deprivation, they can turn out to be sicker than that. In the old days the very sick ones were hospitalized. Now we save money by letting them sleep on the streets.

Some emotionally deprived babies don't even have the means to survive as mentally ill adults. They become physically ill and die. Wouldn't it be wonderful if the Right-to-Lifers put their clout into ensuring *quality* life? It can be done, and it would cost billions less than *Star Wars*.

Jane was saved by her innate talents, especially the ability to keep reaching out. It is as though she felt that if the world wouldn't come to her, she would go out to it. This kept her from becoming what is sometimes called an *introvert*.

A baby also needs to be seduced into developing skills. Those who are talked to tend to talk early. They also tend to hone their thinking machinery, to notice more, to remember, to put thoughts together, to enjoy interacting. Psychologists use words like *perception, motility, judgment,* and *object relations* to name these skills.

That last one, *object relations*, is a clinker. It means, roughly, the ability to form human relationships. So why don't they say it in English? Because scientific language has to be precise. The rough meaning is good enough for our purposes, but not when researchers are working out exactly what's what.

All normal babies have the potential to develop the skills so essential for getting along in the world. But it's clear now, if it wasn't before, that they develop best with encouragement. If babies are left too much to their own devices, the devices have to be better than average for babies to be able to develop on their own. That was the case with Jane. Some babies don't make it. Others, like Jane, don't become all they could be.

Considering the odds, Jane did rather well. She didn't become introverted or pseudoretarded. She kept reaching out and managed to thrive on the crumbs. But the hunger was never sated. And as she grew older, it became entangled with her normal sexual feelings. She couldn't tell the apples from the potatoes. Was she longing for affection, recognition, encouragement, love, or did she really want sex?

Time was people thought that females didn't have sexual desire. That's one past tense to celebrate. Some people think it has gone to the other extreme and that now some women are oversexed. There's no such thing as oversexed. Through sex, one can satisfy all kinds of emotional hunger—to be loved, held, cuddled, wanted. If those are in short supply, as was true with Jane, the need for sex appears to be insatiable. Sex, especially these days, is a socially acceptable vehicle that transports a multitude of needs.

It didn't work that way for Jane. She got to the point where she didn't know when she wanted what. It affected her marriage because, by then, she felt so guilty about her normal sexual needs that she couldn't tolerate even ordinary affection. She became the opposite of oversexed. Her guilt made her frigid. We're beginning to talk about a leading cause of sexual dysfunction here, but there are more. A symptom like that always has more than one cause.

We saw how, as a child, Jane fell into the arms of anyone who wanted to hug her—the butcher, the baker, the candlestick maker. This is not good, not only because of the danger of falling into the wrong pair of arms. Jane escaped that disaster by sheer luck. But her need for affection spread her too thin. Where the ability to love is concerned, we are better off if we keep our eggs in just a few baskets. To love everybody and anybody indiscriminately makes it hard to love very deeply. It wasn't really love, anyway, just emotional hunger.

Jane did love. She loved her mother even though she didn't want to. Children have no choice. They can't shop for the world's best caregiver, so they take what they get. We love for our emotional survival. It has little or nothing to do with whether love is deserved.

Although Jane loved her mother, she didn't like her. That's why she had to become so much like her.

Hold everything! Don't we become like those we love? Yes and no. A little bit of becoming like them is a good thing, especially if we truly admire them. Jane didn't admire her mother at all, so becoming like her was overdone. It protested and protected. It protested too much to conceal her dislike. And, as we shall see, it protected magically by keeping Mother inside, where she would be safe from harm.

Jane also loved her father. When she reached the ages of three, four, five, that love became intertwined with her normal sexuality. Children do become sexually aroused quite naturally. If it's a boy, you can see it. Girls act strangely and, if you are not too inhibited to want to know, that's why.

When Freud "discovered" childhood sexuality in 1905, his medical colleagues were shocked. They didn't know about it because men, in those days, didn't concern themselves with child rearing. They never went near the nursery and kitchen. It is said that European men of that era bragged about not knowing where the kitchen was in their homes. So Freud, by his own admission, discovered what every nursemaid already knew: children are sexy.

We've all heard about the Oedipus complex. It's normal in children at ages three, four, five, six. It only becomes a problem if it enters the unconscious unchanged and thus persists into adulthood. Then it gets in the way.

According to the Greek myth, the infant Oedipus was left to die because the Oracle predicted that he would grow up to murder his father. A kindly shepherd found the baby and gave him to another king to raise as his son. When he became an adult, he got into his hotrod chariot and drove to his real parents' kingdom. En route, he got into an argument with another charioteer over the right of way and killed him without knowing (read, unconsciously) that he was his father.

The riddle of the Sphinx was causing a lot of grief to the inhabitants of that kingdom. Oedipus solved it and was rewarded with the hand of the widowed queen in marriage. No one knew that she was his mother. Again, unconscious.

If you go to Greece, take the tour bus from Athens to Delphi, which is a splendid trip in its own right. Somewhere along the way, the tour guide (especially if he or she is a university student on a summer job) will ask the driver to stop at a crossroads and will tell you that this is where Oedipus and his father had their fatal encounter. Don't believe it. Greek students are understandably fond of their myths. But it *is* a myth. It never happened. Besides, they didn't have paved roads in ancient Greece. Seems they did have the same traffic problems we have now, though.

Myths represent universal wishes that are articulated for us by our literary geniuses. The ancient Greeks seem to have known all about the too-young child's interest in the parent of the opposite sex. Socrates wrote of it in the form of a play entitled *Oedipus Rex*. Freud had to rediscover it all over again around the turn of the twentieth century, because the Victorians had swept sex entirely under the rug. But there were huge bumps on the floors in Victorian households. They practiced sex quite a lot, licitly and otherwise. If they hadn't, Europe would be under-populated now.

Shakespeare knew about the Oedipus complex long before Freud. Reread *Hamlet*. It's all there, including the unconscious guilt in a heavy dose.

The most conservative psychoanalysts (usually referred to as *orthodox* by those who want to deride them as old-fashioned and rigid) think that the Oedipus complex arises full-blown between the ages of three and six. Modern psychoanalysts (called *ego psychologists*) don't disparage orthodoxy because there's more to it than is appreciated these days. But they also realize that a lot of living takes place before the age of three. Orthodox theory plus ego psychology equals modern psychoanalytic theory. Ego psychology has to do with psychological development from the first few days, weeks, months, and years of life onward.

Jane's longing for ordinary affection coincided with her normal oedipal wishes, which coincided with the failure of her parents' marriage, which coincided with her father's loneliness. If he had been getting it, as they say, from her mother, Jane's childish wishes would have had their day and been put to rest. As it was, they didn't have a chance to rest. As we have already seen with Bill, fantasies that are fed remain alive and build even as they go underground.

While Dad was telling her what an inadequate wife Mother was, Mom was telling her what a philanderer Dad was. Jane knew all that without having to be told. Each parent was trying to get love and sympathy from her. Dad even told her how warm the other women were. Jane was rocked by that. She wanted to be what the other women were to him so that he wouldn't need them. Her parents were asking for more than a child can provide.

Jane was disappointed when her parents divorced. She had been hoping that they might get together again. That sounds contradictory in view of Jane's oedipal wishes, until we take into account that children are only free to fantasize in comfort when there is absolute assurance that there is no chance that their wishes will come true. The best assurance is an intact parental marriage.

Divorce devastates children. Everyone knows that, but few know precisely why. Sure, they lose out on the advantages of having an intact family, the visitation arrangements are never satisfactory, and they are often left in poverty because judges tend to favor men. But the real reason divorce is so terrible for children is that the unconscious wishes come dangerously close to being realized, or so it appears to the child.

This is not to say that divorce should never be. Sometimes it is the lesser evil, such as when a parent is psychotic, violent, overtly incestuous, harms the spouse and children physically or emotionally. Jane's parents' marriage was in bad trouble, but professional help probably could have saved it. Dad's needs could have been put in their proper place. Mother's depression could have been cured. There was enough good will, but they didn't know how to give it the right turn.

So Jane's oedipal fantasies built like a fire being fanned. They became all too real when her parents separated because it then appeared that there was a chance the wishes might come true. That does no child any good. It made Jane anxious and guilty beyond endurance. She thought her chances were improving all the time, and it terrified her.

Jane's oedipal fantasies had begun long before her parents separated. Separation merely reinforced them, lent them credence, intensified the guilt. With her mother out of the picture, Jane might be in. Strong stuff for a little girl.

Using ego psychology—the psychology of how the ego develops from birth on—we see that Jane had a hard life before age three. She lived in an emotionally impoverished climate. She sensed that, as the second child, she should have been a boy. Her fantasies built around the theme that there was something wrong with her.

She noticed, as all children do, that boys have something she didn't have. Bill got over that shock because he had it. For Jane, though, it became the focus of her poor self-esteem.

Freud's concept of penis envy is very much in disrepute these days. People have a tendency to discard what they do not like. But the objectors are only partly right. Girls (and women who unconsciously retain girlhood wishes) do not literally want a penis. They fasten onto the idea because children think concretely. They feel a vague longing that can't be put into words. If it could be, they would say, "I feel the need for more affection, or recognition, or affirmation than I'm getting." But children cannot know that. They can only feel that something is missing. Then, if the child is a girl, she sees a penis for the first time. That must be it! If it's a boy, he doesn't have that hook to hang his unhappiness on. Maybe that's worse.

Now we've come to a second cause of Jane's frigidity. Add "penis envy" to guilt. The childish reasoning here is that she lacks the proper instrument with which to function sexually.

A third cause. In her unconscious mind, every man represented her father. Remember, nobody wants oedipal wishes to come true. So Jane had to prevent it by not allowing it to happen, as though it could.

A fourth. As those wishes threatened to come true, the complete fantasy required that her mother, sister, and stepmother be dead. This went beyond guilt. It involved her love for them in conflict with those death wishes. This is why the overwhelming majority of true neurotics do not become violent. Love tempers the other wishes. You've got to be much sicker than merely neurotic to become violent.

We've just defined mental illness as involving the inability to love. That's not the whole story, only a large part of it.

We've also just described again what psychoanalysts mean by *neurotic conflict*. But you don't need my explanation. The poets always say it better. Hamlet was so immobilized by a conflict like Jane's that he delayed taking action, found it hard to kill, had to be killed in the end as punishment for his unconscious guilt.

There are even more reasons for Jane's ending up preferring too little out of life. Emotional starvation from birth onward supplied the first threads that set the basic pattern for her tapestry. Next came the restraint when she needed to toddle around, adding more threads to the same pattern, quelling whatever spark of self-esteem she might have had. Don't strive too much. Don't think you're so great. Don't try to achieve. Jane got those messages early and well.

Children are better off thinking they are great. A friend of mine remarked about someone he disliked, "He's an insufferable narcissist." I asked, "Have you ever known a sufferable narcissist?" "Sure," he said, "A two-year-old." He was right. Happy two-year-olds are in love with themselves and their worlds; they think no one has ever before performed the feats they are just learning. And we love to watch them preen. When we grow up, we can no longer behave that way and get away with it (unless we are Mayor of New York City).

Now it's becoming even clearer what ego psychology is all about. The ego has to be built in childhood. In adulthood, it has to yield to more realistic self-evaluation. We are not as great as we thought we were when we were children. But it was a wonderful and necessary feeling while it lasted.

Jane started life with a short supply of "sufferable" narcissism. The guilt came later. There has to be a conscience—or *superego* in psychoanalytic jargon—before there can be a guilty one. We are not born with a conscience. It has to develop. With some people it doesn't. We have to lock them up if we can catch them.

As soon as Jane had a conscience, she had a guilty one. Her fantasies violated all of the Commandments. She didn't really commit any of those sins, of course; she only wished.

It's not only children who believe that a thought is as bad as a deed. President Jimmy Carter was forced by his conscience to confess publicly that he lusted after women. Other people are more liberal about it. They believe that when you stop lusting, you're dead.

Unconscious guilt is never about real crimes. It often happens, when a crime is committed, that innocent people rush to the police to confess. They have to seek punishment even though the crime is only in their fantasies. They give the police the trouble of having to prove that they are not the perpetrators; otherwise the grand juries would be kept too busy.

Jane lusted, coveted, and murdered in fantasy. That's why she had to spend her life worrying about her mother. She was afraid her childhood death wishes would come true. In order to live her own life, she couldn't keep an eye on Mother all the time. A good unconscious device in such circumstances is to *become* Mother. Then you've got her where you can see her. It's good for counteracting guilt. It's not so good for being yourself and living your own life.

This touches on another flaw in the role model idea. A person is not like a Vogue pattern. We cannot decide to be like this one and not like that one. Of course, we do become like other people to a greater or lesser extent. But it is a creative process that takes place outside our awareness. Psychoanalysts call it *identification.* The creative part goes beyond mere copying. It involves taking some of the other person, and a lot of ourselves, to make a unique personality.

Jane thought of her mother as a negative role model and determined, consciously, that she would never be like her. Many such determinations have been defeated by unconscious needs such as Jane's. Jane needed to keep her mother alive and well and living within her.

I said that Jane's neurotic symptom was frigidity. But it was broader than that. Preference for too little out of life was her psychological solution to many problems—low self-esteem; disapproval of exploration, striving, initiative; sexual fantasies; rivalry; and death wishes. And guilt, tons of guilt.

You see now why the mechanical solutions of sex therapy don't solve the problem. It's like plucking weeds while leaving the roots. They don't show for a while, but they're still alive and they grow back. When her guilt became intolerable, Jane did not go to the police. What she did instead was squelch the desire for pleasure, both in and out of bed.

Psychologists call that a *compromise solution.* At last we have a technical term that anyone can understand. *Compromise* in psychological jargon has the same meaning as it does in everyday language. It is the best one can get in less-than-perfect circumstances. It gives something in order to get something. Jane gave up pleasure. What she got was an uneasy peace.

When Jane became an adult, she couldn't engage in healthy competition. With a superior education, she was content to go into a typing pool. Even when some kind soul encouraged her out of it, she couldn't allow herself to compete in the marketplace.

In becoming her mother, Jane was compelled to repeat her mother's marital failure. It didn't have to be. Jane needed help to become her own person. Then Al might have stayed. After all, she was pretty, intelligent, altogether not a bad person. He probably didn't do better with Elaine in the long run.

What could have made a difference in Jane's life? It's the lucky baby who gets grown-up parents. Jane's parents were young, fun loving, and unprepared for parenthood when they married. More emotionally competent parents can love a child when they get to know him or her. They may not have wanted one just then, or it may be one of the wrong sex, but such feelings are overcome by love if there is enough of it.

There is a fiction, promoted with the best of intentions, that "wanted" babies are loved more than "accidental" ones. The fact is that one can want a baby without knowing what it will be like when the baby arrives. Some prepartum fantasies are that it will all be wonderful. The baby will be sweet and cuddly and loving. When the reality arrives and it turns out to be hard work and little sleep, the fantasy is shattered.

It's especially hard on those who need to be loved by the baby. In the beginning, you're lucky when you get that first smile. All you get in the first few weeks is too little sleep and lots of diapers. So the "wanted" baby is not always what was wanted in fantasy.

On the other hand, mature parents can love a baby they didn't plan for. It depends much more on whether they are psychologically up to it than whether they planned it. The best scenario is to want a baby knowing what you are in for and being able to get your satisfaction from the marriage instead of expecting it from the baby. Oddly enough, the baby is more likely to respond when you are not desperate for it.

What could have been done about Jane's family? There is an idea called *primary prevention*. One such setup has the mother or, preferably, both parents come with the baby and discuss how daily life goes. A professional skilled in ego psychology can prevent a lot before it happens.

Example. It could have been noticed that Jane was understimulated—underseduced, as I have called it. How can you make a depressed mother coo at her baby? Show her that it has its rewards. A baby who coos back might get through to a mildly depressed mother. That won't make a dent in a very severe depression. But the "preventor" would take that into account and attempt to do something about it. It's worth a try to break the vicious cycle. If Jane's mother could have been less depressed and more attractive, her father might have been more interested in home life. That would have been one way to have prevented the divorce.

Then, also, a therapist could have helped Jane's father deal with his disappointment in having another girl. The minister did his best, but yielding to God's will doesn't always help a man yield in good grace. Jane's father needed a little nudge, a startup, to find that girls can be rewarding too. Maybe the tack to take there would have been to help him find some enjoyment in the unfolding of Jane's intellectual skills. That would have been far better, less seductive, than his enjoyment of her good looks and childish femininity.

About the strapping into the highchair and stroller at a time when a child has to explore the world. A primary preventor could have encouraged Jane's mother to turn her loose, perhaps by showing her that it could be fun for her, doing it with her at first to be supportive.

These are examples of devices that can turn things around. Parents are people too. What is proposed to them has to be rewarding. Nothing is gained by scolding, but showing them that there can be pleasure in parenting does work. For the child, it can be crucial, because a "primary preventor" knows the critical times in a child's development when a small change can make a large difference. And it's gravy when, as sometimes does happen, it succeeds in solving the parents' problems too.

Chapter 6

A Good Beginning

Eleanor grew up on a dairy farm in New Hampshire, in a family of four boys and three girls. The boys, when they were old enough, worked the farm with their father and three hired hands, at first after school and later full time. The girls, when they were old enough, worked the kitchen with their mother.

There was a hearty breakfast for all at six in the morning. The farm hands took all their meals with the family. Bread had to be started at four; hot cereal was started the night before. There were also pancakes, bacon and ham, eggs, milk, butter, cream, homemade jams for the bread, cheese, and a gallon of steaming black coffee. Farm work takes fuel.

The girls brought in the wood for the stove, served, made sandwiches for the bag lunches for the men and boys to take to the field and for the children to take to school, washed the dishes, went off to school. Their mother scrubbed the pots, cleaned the kitchen, started the roast for dinner. Dinner was as big a deal as breakfast. A roast, big as a fourth of a cow, or a huge stew, or a load of pork chops, or several chickens, potatoes, corn in season, vegetables, fresh bread and pies baked in the afternoon, plenty of butter, milk, cream. There was always enough food, but it had to be worked for.

After dinner, Mother and the girls cleaned up. Father did his accounts. The children did their homework. There was family interaction of sorts, despite the fact that they were doing their separate chores with neither time nor inclination for intimacy. Nevertheless, there was something that is so lacking in many families—this thing called *structure*. The children felt they belonged to something. There was a sense that everyone was doing what he and she was supposed to be doing, fitting into an overall plan. When ten o'clock came, the parents didn't need the nightly news to ask whether they knew where their children are. They were in bed. So were the parents.

Eleanor was the third child, after a boy and a girl. In addition to the cooking, housekeeping, and vegetable garden, their mother also had babies to tend in the early years. She had an occasional helper, especially when the children were very young. As soon as they were old enough, the girls helped with the babies after school.

It sounds as though the women's work was hard. It was. So was the men's. The women didn't think of themselves as exploited. Their work was appreciated as part of the teamwork. The farm couldn't function without them. Sure, the girls became restless in their teenage years. So did the boys. Their world began to seem too small then. But as youngsters, if they thought about the wider world at all, they thought of it as somewhere out there, beyond the next county. As teenagers, if they were frightened of the larger world, they didn't let themselves know it. The urge to get away washed away fear in many. In others, fear of the wider world kept them close to home.

When Eleanor was born, she slept in her parents' room. So did the babies before and after her. No one thought it should be otherwise. That's where the crib was, and their mother could not be expected to go to another room to feed a baby in the middle of a

New Hampshire winter night. The youngest slept in the crib until the next baby came. When Eleanor was three and a half, she was put into the double bed with her sister.

Did Eleanor see the next baby conceived? If she'd been asked, she could have told you all about sex even though few children ever remember their parents' sex. There's no point in asking them later on. Unless it happens during adolescence, it's forgotten so thoroughly that it's even hard to dig up during psychoanalysis. We don't like to think of our parents that way. When pressed, we acknowledge that our parents had sex as many times as there are children. That means they worked at it purposefully, never for the sheer pleasure of it. Yes, Eleanor saw, but she didn't remember. That doesn't mean it didn't register somewhere.

Parents aside, farm children learn about sex earlier and with more visual demonstration than city children. The animals are doing it all around them. And the talk was rough. The men didn't have the time, nor did it occur to anyone as necessary, to save their talk for when the children weren't present. Mealtime was meeting time. The distribution of chores was discussed. If a cow was calving, the job of looking after her was assigned at the table. It went along with talk about when to plow and who would tend to the milking. Mating the animals and calving them was just another farm chore like all the rest. Some of the talk was pretty crude, but it was not intentionally so. The so-called facts of life were all around them. Mating animals was no different from sowing seed. The very business of a farm is reproduction, when you look at the bottom line.

Their mother didn't tell the girls anything about sex. She probably thought there was nothing left to tell by the time they would have asked. She was partly right, but they did need to hear something from her, regardless of what they had seen the animals doing. They needed to know something about love so that people mating would not be thought of as the same as animal mating. And who belonged with whom? Was everyone fair game for everyone else, or was that only true for the animals? The young animals were protected from mating too soon. What about people? Nothing was ever said.

By anyone's standards, this was a good, God-fearing, stick-together family. They didn't believe in a lot of talk in general, so it didn't appear that sex was especially omitted. While they talked about animals freely, they never talked about human relationships. They wouldn't have known what that meant. If you'd asked them, they would have thought that *relationship* referred to their relatives who lived on nearby farms. It would not have occurred to these stolid, undemonstrative New Englanders that something had to be said about love, or that love could be expressed demonstrably.

Not only did Eleanor's parents have no time for individual child cuddling, but they also wouldn't have been comfortable doing it. Again, if you'd have asked, they'd have said that of course they love their children, but such questions would have embarrassed them. Love wasn't something to talk about. Eleanor was loved New England fashion: She was there because she was born to them, accepted without question. That's more love than there is in many families. But Eleanor didn't know much about how love feels. The best she could have answered, had anyone asked such an unlikely question, is that it feels like belonging. That's not nothing, but she didn't feel special. She was one of the litter.

The nudity that was practiced by city people as "natural" was unknown on the farm. Everyone covered up—the adults, that is. Children were different. Hot water was hard to come by. They were all put into the bathtub together.

Babies were born at home. The local doctor came, as well as one or another of the aunts from nearby farms. A hired woman took over the mother's kitchen job until she was on her feet again. The older kids were sent off to an aunt's farm for the delivery; in those days, that meant they were gone for two weeks or so. They doubled up in their cousins' rooms. There was sex play, group play as well as coupling off in private. They invented games. In one game, the boys were in a room with bathrobes held open. The girls were in another room. At a signal, the girls were allowed in. If they came quickly enough, they would catch a boy with his robe open. It was exciting. The boys were quicker. They were hardly ever caught. The excitement didn't bother anyone. The adults were working. The neighbors were miles away.

Not one of those kids didn't know what the other sex looked like. But knowing doesn't have the charge of experiencing, for any of us, which is really terrific when you stop to think about it. Imagine sitting home with all that knowledge instead of going after some excitement. Life would be drab. Kids do not play sex games for educational purposes, even though showing and looking are a large part of what they do.

There were other games, like group masturbation. There were also private things. A boy and girl would get into one of the bedrooms and put a chair against the door. They would examine each other's genitals. Often they would try putting them together, with varying degrees of success when they were very young. When they were older, success came with frantic fear of pregnancy. One boy cousin was particularly fond of Eleanor, and they always paired off together when they had the chance. When they got older they stopped, not only because of fear of pregnancy; sex with cousins was too close to incest to be comfortable.

Farm kids engage in the same sex play as city kids, for the same reason. Children have a healthy interest in sex. So do farmhands. The unhealthy part is that the farmhands have only the farmer's daughters (and sons) to fool around with on weekdays. There are jokes about that, but it's not funny for the kids. A girl goes out for wood and encounters a farmhand exhibiting himself behind the woodshed. Here's another place where knowing all about it is in the brain but not in the emotions. A young girl becomes aroused and confused about her feelings. Rarely would a farmhand rape a girl because pregnancy would get him into serious trouble in that small community. Unfortunately for the boys, they were fair game.

Eleanor's parents were conservative and reticent. Children rarely turn to their parents when they are molested. They feel too guilty because they have become aroused. For Eleanor, it was out of the question. She knew it would create all kinds of issues that nobody could handle. To begin with, starting such a conversation meant talking about a taboo subject. It would have made her parents uncomfortable. The children also knew that the farmhands could not be fired easily. They were too important to the family's livelihood.

Had the parents known, they probably would have punished them in their own fashion. In Eleanor's family, that would have meant taking the culprit to the minister for a scolding. In another farm family, the father might have beat the daylights out of the farmhand. But the more important point is that they didn't want to talk about such things, and Eleanor didn't want to embarrass them.

Since the parents grew up on farms, didn't they know what happens? Yes and no. It was repressed, tucked away. New Englanders are not the only people who don't want to hear things they would rather not know.

The aunt who came to help with a baby's birth never stayed very long. She had her own farm to work. When she left, the kids came back. Eleanor watched her mother and sister take care of the next brother. He became hers in her fantasies long before she became old enough to take care of him. When he did become "hers," she imagined all sorts of things. She was his mother. Who was his father? She buried that one fast. Her brother's penis was hers, she let herself imagine. She could play with it without being noticed while she took care of him. It was like playing with herself, in a way. Her devotion to him grew. It was looked upon as a virtue. She enjoyed being thought of as a good sister. It gave her some longed-for distinction, relieved her ache for recognition—

somewhat. Led her to her life's work, although she didn't know that yet.

Eleanor's father was as good a father as he had time to be. That meant not much more than reading from the Bible on Sundays. He was working for them, wasn't he? He had little or no time for the children individually, especially the girls. He didn't have to make time for the boys. They were with him all day working the farm. The girls were closer to their mother, for the same reason. Eleanor would have preferred being a boy. There seemed to be more advantages. In secret, she was, because she had usurped her little brother's penis in her imagination. Over the years it became a secret between them, not that he knew what her fantasies were. He had his own. The shared secret was that she had to put him to bed because he couldn't get to sleep without her fondling him. The family didn't know that part. Everyone thought it was sweet.

After putting her little brother to bed and finishing her homework, Eleanor got into the big bed where her older sister also slept. That's where she belonged. There were four bedrooms in the farmhouse—one for the parents, one for the girls, two for the boys. Eleanor slept on the side of the bed near the wall. When the third girl was moved from the crib, the oldest sister got her own single bed in the same room. The youngest one got to sleep in Eleanor's spot. Eleanor moved to the outside of the bed so that the little one wouldn't fall off. When the cousins came because *their* mother was having a baby, everyone doubled up. Eleanor never slept alone.

Eleanor's older sister married a boy from another farm when Eleanor was sixteen. That left more work for the other girls. Eleanor remained at home for a year after high school. Then she went to New York to attend nursing school.

She told her parents that the year at home was to help out. Actually, she was seeing a young man she knew from high school. He'd come around in his family's pickup and take her out—movies, dancing, sex in the truck. She thought she might marry him and remain in farming. They didn't exactly quarrel, but a feeling of friction grew up between them. Eleanor could not have said then what the trouble was. Years later she knew. Something about the narrowness of living forever in the county in which she was born began to feel intolerable. She longed for something more. Dan didn't understand. He wanted her precisely because she fit in so well with the life-style that he was going to perpetuate.

Nursing school was a good getaway. Her parents wondered why it had to be New York; there were nursing schools in New England. But they didn't try to stop her.

She didn't leave her mother in the lurch. Women were hired to help. The farm was prospering in those days, and the parents did not try to hold the children back, at least not deliberately. The boys went to the agricultural college. Eleanor was the first girl to go away. Her sister's marriage had not been regarded as "away." But no one disapproved openly. Whatever feelings her parents had about her leaving were washed away by the rationalization that nursing is a noble profession. They were not given to struggling with complex feelings. Although nothing was said, Eleanor felt a certain tug, a longing for them to say they were sorry to see her go. They couldn't bring themselves to say that, although everyone knew that, except for visits, she'd never come back to the farm.

The farm had not prepared Eleanor for New York, but she didn't have to take the plunge too suddenly. The students' residence at the nursing school was wide world enough, yet protective because the rules were strict. In fact, because of the structure, it was a good transition from home. The students were all kinds of people from all over. Eleanor learned a lot about the heterogeneous world – different races, religions, economic strata, political outlooks, how people who were not farmers lived.

She was better equipped than many for the heavy workload at nursing school. She had worked like that all her life, so she did well. And there was a bit of social life, dances a few times a year – Halloween, Thanksgiving, before going home for Christmas.

The dances and parties were not easy at first because Eleanor didn't know what to talk about. Back home everyone talked about familiar things. City people weren't interested in farming, although some never missed an opportunity to sneer at it. Someone asked her whether she knew how to call hogs. At first she answered innocently that there are mostly cows on a dairy farm. It took her a while to catch on to urban superiority. It took another while for her to realize that they were really envious of the security of farm life.

There were a few male nursing students. Eleanor stuck with them because she knew them from classes. They weren't exactly dates, just good to go out with in a group. And she was still not completely over Dan. She saw him when she went home for the holidays. She still liked him, but she was not tempted to settle down like that, especially after New York.

The nursing students took group forays to places like the Broadway theatres when they could afford the splurge. Once or twice they went to a disco. They couldn't do that too often because of the hours. They had to sign out and in at the residence and be on their feet all of the day after.

When Eleanor graduated from nursing school, life speeded up for her. It went too fast. She had a few affairs with some medical students. They took her to more sophisticated places, like Lincoln Center and some of the posh restaurants. Some took her to their families' homes. She began to see how people lived off the farm. She learned about apartment dwelling and about surburban life in houses that bore no resemblance to a farmhouse. It was an eye opener. Some of these men had mothers with careers. At first they appeared to her like creatures from outer space. Mostly, though, she spent time with her men friends in their apartments.

Nothing ever came of these affairs. She was attractive enough to be able to find men almost at will. The hospital was full of them—students, physicians, technicians, detailers. One affair followed another. Finally she got into a long-term relationship with Joe, a surgery resident. The future looked bright. But he never committed himself. There was a difference in religion. Eleanor didn't mind, and her family would have been too awed to have minded. But it never came to that. He couldn't quite tell her that his family would mind. In fact, he couldn't tell his family about her. Kept putting it off. A couple of years dragged by. Eleanor began to realize that it wouldn't come off.

She resumed dating, anyone and everyone. Dan was long for-gotten, and now she had to keep going to try to forget Joe. She was getting nowhere but exhausted. The singles' bars were scary. She didn't want to go home with a sex maniac. That's when some of the nurses took her to a women's bar. She was willing to try anything. She allowed herself to be picked up, went home with the woman, was sick the next day over what she had let her-self in for.

In a way, it was sobering. She decided to stop the whirlwind of one-night stands with anybody and everybody. In her worse moments she thought that maybe life with Dan would not have been so bad. In her better moments she knew she would have been bored out of her mind. So what? She was bored now. There were fewer eligible men. She passed child-bearing age. Not much to look forward to except a life of devotion to her patients. She was destined to be the older sister to her little brother forever.

Chapter 7

Why It Wasn't Good Enough

Now that we are familiar with the subtle seductions, it isn't hard to enumerate those that affected Eleanor. What is hard is to say which of them could have been prevented and how that could have been done. After all, Eleanor grew up in a better-than-ordinary home in an intact family that was far above the poverty level.

By now it is clear that one or two events that might be thought of as subtly seductive don't matter. They begin to matter as they combine with other, similar events *and* with the fantasies that weave them all together. This bears repetition because, when Freud was in the process of discovering psychoanalysis, he first thought that a single traumatic childhood event accounted for adult neurosis. Many people still believe that, although Freud himself and the psychoanalysts who came after him abandoned the idea many years ago.

The events, the emotional climate within which they are experienced, plus the fantasies, are what add up to something. And that something needn't turn out to be detrimental. If there is

talent, it can be the stuff that is turned into something useful—
into useful work at least. If the talent is great enough, it can be
turned into art or music or literature. In Eleanor's case it turned
into a professional skill.

At what cost to Eleanor? There is always a reckoning.
Eleanor went to her goal of service to others as though in a
straight line. Why? Because that was where the rewards had
been all her life. Reward for nursing was like a built-in promise.
We all seek (and if we are lucky, find) our own roads to glory, to
where the payback looks promising.

Here is the issue of the unconscious again. It dictates our behavior in ways that some of us would rather not believe. Since
Freud discovered the Oedipus complex, few have disputed that
the unconscious has an influence upon marital choice. But career
choice? Yes. Unconscious fantasies and wishes influence many of
our decisions and choices, large and small.

So far as choice of vocation goes, if that were not so, we'd all go
where the money is, if we could get there. The shortest road to
riches is still to have had a great-grandfather who discovered oil,
or built a railroad, or founded a bank. If we have to do it ourselves,
we need an M.B.A. or a place in the trading pit. But not everyone
can do that. Even the everyones who are equipped with the education and the smarts can't all crowd into Wall Street, which,
after all, consists of a few small city blocks. The financial wizards
are there because they like it. We can't live happily doing something we don't like. If we can, we choose something that will be
emotionally satisfying. That's where the unconscious comes in,
because part of that decision is based on what the unconscious has
found satisfying before. Not all of us have such wide choices, of
course. Some of us have to do work we don't like and, if we're
lucky, take an early retirement.

Eleanor needed to be appreciated for providing a service to
others. That's how she experienced her place in the family. Her
parents accepted her because she was there. That's not enough
for a child. Children have to feel special in some way. Since it was

not given to her, Eleanor gave it to herself. She took what was there—being valued for service—and turned it into something more meaningful to her. Helping her mother and "nursing" her brother became her life's work. It made her a good nurse. Question is, did it make her a happy woman?

Turning a situation into something meaningful is called *adaptation* by psychoanalytic psychologists. We know about adaptation from biology. Animals adapt to their environments. In a cold climate, they grow fur. The human animal is not quite so adaptive, biologically. In a cold climate, the human has to steal the animal's fur.

To notice psychological adaptation requires a closer look. We all know people who have made the best of terrible situations. I don't mean martyrs or masochists. I mean those who have truly turned things around for themselves. Good adapters survive in all but the most destructive environments. Adaptation doesn't work if the baby does its utmost but there's no response. Even the best adapters have to give up if the circumstances are too defeating. Eleanor adapted because she had a gift for adaptation *and* because the family situation was not all that bad. Compared with many, it was superior. What were Eleanor's subtle seductions, then?

She slept in her parents' room at first, and in her sister's bed later. Why do I keep dwelling on sleeping arrangements?

Ideally, a child should have a room of his or her own. This is not because parents have intercourse every night. And when they do, it can be (and has been) argued that children are asleep and don't notice. Anyone who has been psychoanalyzed will tell you otherwise.

People think children are asleep when they aren't. Even partly asleep, they see and hear more than we think. Psychologists have a term for observation of parental intercourse. They call it the *primal scene*. Everybody has a primal scene, even if they haven't been present at it. We have it in our fantasy of what the parental relationship is like. Many children think of it as a fight. If they actually see it, it looks that way to them. If they only imagine it, they base their fantasies upon what they see about the parents' relationship in the daytime. If they fight, it's a fight. If they're loving, it's loving. In Eleanor's fantasy it was probably another chore, like spring planting.

How do we know with such certainty that these experiences and fantasies exist if children don't remember? One way is that we "uncover" them—that is, revive the memory—in psychoanalytic treatment. One of Freud's famous cases is popularly known as the "Wolf Man" because he had a dream of wolves peering with wide-open eyes. Freud analyzed this dream and found that the Wolf Man had indeed witnessed the primal scene in infancy. He was the son of a Russian nobleman who fled to Vienna because of the Russian revolution. Not only poor children sleep in the parental bedroom. What this amounts to is, if it can't be helped it can't. If it can be helped, help it.

There was the shocking story, some years ago, of a woman murdered in a well-lit parking lot late at night. The killer stalked her with a knife for almost an hour before he did her in. Thirty-eight people living in an apartment building overlooking the lot watched in fascination the entire time. No one phoned the police, although they could have done so anonymously. They merely stared in horror. Reporters, essayists, moralists, criminologists, and philosophers have pondered this, trying to understand what immobilized so many people.

The reason they couldn't report it, in my opinion, is not that they were as callous as they appear. Rather, it reminded them of the long forgotten primal scene of their childhoods. The memories were only partial, however. Hardly anyone remembers the event. More usually, only the emotions are remembered. That is, the part of the memory that contains the scene is forgotten; the feelings that accompanied the scene are remembered and tacked onto something similar years later. Psychoanalysts call that *isolation*. Those witnesses to the murder on the parking lot were re-

membering the horrible fascination. Why didn't they report it?
No one reports their parents to the police, except in Russia.

Even if you engage in sex only once a week or once a month or
once a year, your very life in the same room with the child, aside
from sex, is more exciting than the child needs. "What!" you will
argue, "My child likes us to be there, has trouble sleeping without
us." Children love to be in their parents' rooms, especially in their
beds. It's fun as a special treat. It's too much of a good thing if it
becomes the rule rather than the exception. People have to learn
to be alone and like it. They learn it while growing up, if given the
chance.

Most children in the world sleep in their parents' rooms out of
necessity. Many families in this less-than-perfect world don't
even have a room. In India, children sleep in their parents' spots
on the street. If the housing shortage continues, New York won't
be any different from New Delhi.

The basics of food and shelter come before the psychological
"luxuries." But what about a family like Eleanor's? They were not
wealthy, but neither were they poor. They had the *means* but not
the *knowledge* to do better by their children psychologically.

A room of one's own helps one to acquire a sense of self. A
child with a room feels important. "This is *mine.*" Have you noticed how early a child acquires a sense of possession? *Mine* becomes a big word, especially if there are siblings who grab one's
toys. A child with a room is a prince or princess with a kingdom.

Of course, that is frequently impossible. You don't have to go
to India. In New York, space goes for $250 and up a square foot.
Only real kings and ex-dictators can manage that. We are talking
here about the ideal. Approach it as closely as you can. If you can't
reach it, there's no reason to feel guilty. It is possible to compen-
sate by finding other ways to make a child feel special. Eleanor's
parents didn't make her feel special enough in any way. A few minutes a day alone with one or both parents, a time just for her,
might have done it. As it was, she was just one of the girls in the

kitchen. No one special. Same for the boys. They were like the fieldhands, more or less interchangeable.

There are so many ways to create something special. Eleanor could have had a job that her sisters couldn't do—maybe "Eleanor's Special Muffins." Seek out whatever makes your child different from her sister or brother. Is she better at reading? Do a few pages of her own special book with her each day. That doesn't mean neglect the one who is not so good at reading. Read to her separately. She might get better. Does she like word puzzles, math puzzles? Maybe just talk is enough. Take her out on the porch alone for a few minutes. If you have six children, give them ten minutes each. That's an hour out of your evening.

It would have been difficult, in Eleanor's case, for her mother to have had her in another room while she needed to be fed during the night. That's hard for a mother in a warm climate, but worth doing. In a New England winter, it's torture, so we have to do some weighing of one thing against another. A tortured mother is good neither for her own sake nor for the baby's. In this instance, the climate decides what is best.

A very good expedient is some sort of room divider—a curtain or a screen. That is not soundproof, of course, but it does give the child a sense of privacy.

A divider of some sort is also a good idea when traveling. It's difficult do better than that when traveling with a baby or young child. For one thing, the rooms would have to connect, and not all hotels are built that way. For another, they'll think you're crazy to want to pay for a room for a child, even if you can afford it. But if you ask for a screen, there's a good chance they may not call an ambulance to cart you away to the local mental hospital.

There are other ways if you can afford them. A two-room suite can be a good solution. The crib starts in the bedroom and can be wheeled into the other room when you are ready for bed.

Why all the fuss? Suppose you decide to abstain from sex on a brief vacation? Does a baby still need privacy? Doesn't a baby need someone there all the time? Yes and no. A baby needs to be by himself at times. Bedtime is one of those times—probably the most important.

Then there is this thing that people call ego. Children have egos that grow just as their bodies do. They get more than just a temporary charge out of being treated as someone special. I know a parent who paid a fare on the bus for a two-year-old so that she could have her own seat. She preened all the way to the destination. That was money well spent. Good experiences add up just as detrimental ones do. We want to give our children a preponderance of good feelings about themselves. It cushions them when the inevitable bad experiences occur.

Things are far more complex if you have older children, and even more complex if they are of different sexes. But, you will argue, how can a few nights on a vacation make such a big difference? I've already said that one experience doesn't matter. True. But remember the cumulative potential—and ego, the feeling of being important.

Eleanor's family didn't travel, and the crib didn't have to be as stationary as they made it. If they had moved it into another room when she was able to sleep through the night, it would have made some difference.

What else about Eleanor? She didn't have a bed of her own when her parents moved her out of the crib. Many children cannot have beds of their own. Again, give them one wherever possible. Childhood is not all fun and games. There are psychological tasks that promote psychological development. One of the more important of these tasks is to get to know oneself, one's body, the boundaries of one's physical self. A child accomplishes this more readily without the interference of other bodies to blur the boundaries. Some people do not know where their psychological boundaries lie. They always feel incomplete unless someone is psychologically, if not physically, joined to them. They are psychological Siamese twins. Psychologists call them *borderline personalities*. On the other side of the border lies madness.

This is not to say that sleeping with another person in childhood makes a person nearly psychotic. The causes of such severe mental illnesses are vastly more complex than that. Sleeping with a sibling, or whoever, is a hurdle to acquiring a feeling of intactness. Most people can leap over that hurdle if all else is favorable. Why put a hurdle there if it is not an unavoidable necessity?

When Eleanor's little brother was born, many more psychological hazards entered her life. The kids were sent away. The good part is that they knew the extended family so well that they did not have to deal with being sent away to strangers. Still, it was a disruption for them, maybe a necessary one if the baby had to be born at home. If the mother goes to the hospital, the kids should be kept at home whenever there is that option. They need their familiar surroundings.

The bad part of being sent away was that Eleanor was not long past her own infancy. Children at that age do not tolerate long separations from mother. They need her physical presence because she is not yet firmly fixed in their minds. That's why young kids cry when mother goes out of sight. If they can't see her, she doesn't exist. That feeling of having lost her is more devastating than we can imagine. Those loud wails are not for a trivial reason.

But Eleanor, at age three and a half, was with sister, brother, aunt, uncle, cousins. What's the big deal? The big deal is that her mother had truly disappeared from her mind. No one enjoyed her wailing. In their more mature minds, mother still existed and Eleanor was being an unreasonable nuisance. She shut up fast when they mocked her. Shutting up didn't take away the agony.

What did? Snuggling with her sister helped. But that was like a narcotic—useful when there is real but temporary pain, addictive if it goes on.

When the kids got home, there was the baby. *Jealousy*

doesn't do the matter justice. A normally intelligent child realizes before very long that life will never be the same again. That's not all bad. A child does have to move on, can't remain the baby forever. But the arrival of a new member of the family calls for adjustment, even by the adults. It upsets the equilibrium of the unit. Eventually, if all goes well, a new equilibrium is established. It's not easy, especially for a child.

Eleanor made a reasonable adjustment, but it cost her. By secretly becoming the baby's mother, she solved several psychological problems at once. This is not at all unusual in psychological life. A single solution constitutes a net that catches a lot of fish.

Becoming the baby's mother solved the jealousy, maybe a bit too quickly. Eleanor already knew that she couldn't expect much sympathy for being jealous. But when you stop to think about it, why shouldn't a child feel jealous and have those feelings understood? Eleanor's family was uncomfortable with feelings. There certainly was no room for inconvenient ones.

What would it have served if someone, mother or father or both, had listened to how Eleanor felt, let her cry it out, given her special privileges as a reward for being older? It would have helped her gain dimension in her emotional life. Her feelings would have been affirmed. She would have come to believe that there are no wrong, unacceptable feelings. Children need to learn not to act on their feelings, not not to feel them.

What did Eleanor lose? The opportunity to feel right about her emotions. Her stockpile of ego was lessening instead of growing.

By becoming the baby's secret mother, Eleanor also "identified" with her mother. This was much to the good. It firmed down her femininity. That is why, so very many years later, despite her loneliness, she couldn't enjoy making it with a woman. She was secure in her own gender.

However, there is a part of it that was too much of a good thing. It didn't allow her normal rivalry with her mother to blossom and have its day. A girl (and boy) needs to go through a pe-

riod of competition with the parent of the same sex, provided, of
course, that the parent is grown up enough to handle it. When a
girl begins to think that she can do things better than mother, of
course she is kidding herself. But why not let her glory in her self-
deception for a while? The bubble will burst naturally, as she
comes to realize that she's not as big as she feels. Children face reality best in their own sweet time. They don't need bubble burst-
ers coming at them from the outside. They benefit from thinking
big while it lasts. It gives the ego one more boost that doesn't
necessarily get deflated when the child comes to better terms
with the reality that she is still a child, not mother's equal.

What else did becoming the baby's mother solve for Eleanor?
She could pretend that her oedipal wishes were fulfilled. This was
her baby, and we know who his father was. Again, this was both
good and bad for Eleanor – good for her to have such a fantasy.
Better if it had been with a doll. It became too real when responsibility for the baby was turned over to her in a big way. She was
praised so much for it. She was so competent, such a good little
mother. They made it impossible for her to realize that it was only
a fantasy. Of course, they didn't know her fantasy, only that it
was convenient that she took over so much of the baby's care.

We already saw, in Bill's case, that a little girl can hardly keep
her hands off a little boy's penis. It is there, like a doorknob, only
softer to the touch. Normally a child who needs something to
touch for comfort finds it in her "security blanket." Those things
serve a very useful purpose. They provide comfort while the child
is making the transition from being part of mother to becoming
her own self. That purpose is served only if it is a thing. It doesn't
work as a transition when it is a person. For Eleanor, it doomed
her to adult loneliness. No one can have a live person to fondle all
the time.

As we saw with Jane, the oedipal wish is a wish we all harbor,
until it appears to come true. Then it is a disaster. Eleanor had to
do something about that psychologically. She assuaged her guilt
by being as good as gold. She took care of all her chores, including

the baby, stayed out of the way, didn't demand anything special, became conforming, convenient, helpful. She spent the rest of her life doing penance.

The sex play with the cousins added to her guilt. Children normally engage in sex play. It does no harm and a bit of good, *if the play is confined to contemporaries.* It is disastrous if it breaches the generation gap. With one's peers, it is a way of discharging some sexual tension. It doesn't take care of all of it, thank goodness. The residue gets stored away for later. For Eleanor, however, it was one more cog in her guilt machine.

Then came adolescence. Hard on the child. Harder, perhaps, on the parents. Not for Eleanor's parents. She was not likely to give her parents a bit of trouble, ever. So there was no adolescent upheaval—at least not where anyone could see it. The inner turmoil was hers alone to contain.

The farmhands did their little numbers on the girls and boys. There was no one else around, which doesn't excuse what they did, because an older person should never take advantage of a child. We get outraged when they do, and we are right. Why? Because the most precious aspect of childhood is the opportunity to develop normally, in one's own time, in order to be successful with an appropriate partner later on. To impair that is to impair the person's entire future.

The farmhands were not true child molesters. They reasoned that the children knew all about it anyway. In their minds they were only getting some close-to-innocent kicks. They didn't intend harm. What it meant to Eleanor, however, is that she didn't matter much. She was ripe for that because she was already enured to it. And, of course, it was fuel for her guilt.

By the time Eleanor was a young adult, her future was decided. I don't mean her professional choice. Nursing is a fine profession, and we can't have too many good nurses. One can become a nurse and still live a normal life. Eleanor couldn't. She had to bolster her self-esteem by overwork, overdevotion, overpenance.

Eleanor needed all she could get and used the only method

that had ever worked. Stifle feelings, don't ask for too much from life, work hard. So even her need for someone had to be denied. That's the way of penance.

She ended up alone.

Chapter 8

Too Much of a Good Thing

More is not always better. A child needs one home. Those who have no home are in dire straits indeed. Those who have more than one are probably affluent enough to be physically comfortable. Two homes may be better than none, but they are worse than one, because children who have one home too many are usually the children of divorce. Whether custody is shared or only visitation arranged, children are shuttled back and forth. What they need is to live in the same room, sleep in the same bed, have the reassurance of the familiar. This has nothing to do with second homes, vacations, visits to Grandma. In those instances, a child knows where home is.

Bob was the child of divorce. He was also an only child. Some people think that in itself is a trauma. Some only children like it that way because it makes them feel special. Others feel deprived if they have no siblings. In the best of circumstances, siblings are the companions of childhood, the friends of middle age, the sharers of the burden of aging parents. Sometimes siblings are consid-

erably less than that. Maybe the answer is that if you are going to
have siblings, have good, kind, loving, generous ones.

There are myths about why people have only one child. The
most common is that the parents didn't want more children. Underneath that is the implication that they didn't even want that
one. Often that is unjust. Some parents try very hard to have a
child and are lucky if they succeed once. Others have lost children
and are left with one.

Nevertheless, it is true that some have one child and regret it.
Bob's parents didn't regret it. They needed a son to carry on the
family name. If they'd had a girl first, they probably would have
kept on until a son came along. If that had happened, the girl
would have been in another kind of psychological trouble. She'd
have been made to feel she was not good enough. But when a boy
is preferred, he doesn't necessarily have it better. It only looks
that way. We cannot know how people feel from the outside looking in. It's too subjective. Boys who are preferred know that they
haven't done anything to deserve it. That doesn't enhance
self-esteem.

Bob's parents hit it the first time, so they didn't need more
children. Clearly, we are not talking about needing children in order to love them. The purpose of having a child to carry on the
family name is to stroke the paternal ego. That doesn't include
love for the child as an essential part of the undertaking. Bobby
was a prized possession, valued perhaps a tad more than the
prize studs his father kept for breeding race horses.

Bobby's parents didn't need more children because they were
too busy being young socialites. Everyone in their circle had
nurses for their children so that the social schedule would not
miss a beat. There was no way Bobby's mother could have told
her hostess that she couldn't come to dinner that evening because
Bobby was sick. It would have spoiled the table arrangement.
First things first. And if Bobby's mother had decided that she
would raise Bobby herself, she would have been ostracized by her
social set, demoted to the middle class. It simply wasn't done.

Bobby's mother cared a great deal about what was and wasn't done.

Except for the last part of her pregnancy and a short while after delivery, her social schedule went on. Bobby could have done all right with a nanny as his psychological mother. Many children do. In Bobby's case, however, the nannies kept changing. It's not possible for a child to make the kind of solid connection with one person that is so essential to psychological development if the mothering persons constantly change. It's one thing when the tragedies in life necessitate it, but why arrange for it? So it's fine to have a nanny if she is well chosen in the first place, and if she stays. Those are big ifs. What if the nanny you hoped would stay throughout his childhood turns out to be unsuitable, or leaves for her own reasons? Parents have been known to make every kind of concession to get a nanny to stay. It's better for the baby, but it can turn out to be blackmail.

Bobby was bottle fed by the nanny. There is nothing psychologically wrong with bottle feeding if the baby is held. Nutritionally, breast milk is better for the baby. Psychologically, what matters is how it's done.

The holding and close emotional contact during the feeding are the child's first encounters with another person. These experiences lay down unrememberable "memories" that will help the child develop psychologically and even intellectually. Although this can never be recalled in the form of distinct memories, a pattern of confident expectation and self valuation is established by being fed comfortably and predictably each time one is hungry. Children come to value themselves, and later others, out of having had good experiences from the start. And, since we value I.Q.'s so much, it's good to know that the baby's intellectual potential can be developed simply by how we hold him or her. This does not mean, of course, that we can create what is not there. The child brings the potential, which is inborn. It can be developed or retarded by outside influence.

Many years ago, Dr. Spitz entered the controversy about the

Head Start program. While the budget cutters did not want it at all, Dr. Spitz argued that the program comes too late in a child's life. He believed that the first few minutes, days, and weeks of life are so crucial that the child has to be "started up" then. Later is too late. It is through those very early experiences that the child learns how to learn. By that, Dr. Spitz meant that the intellectual capacity is stimulated in conjunction with good self feelings that make for initiative and willingness to learn. But the more important factor is that a baby has to acquire confident interest in the mothering person in order later to be able to expand that interest to the world at large.

One problem with a nursing bottle is that the baby can be held at a distance, or not held at all. There are bottle-propping gadgets that make it possible to feed a baby untouched by human hands. That frees the nurse to go away. After a while, the child can hold the bottle himself. This takes away the intimacy with another person, the physical and emotional closeness that the human infant needs to become a social being. An intimate relationship develops with the bottle instead. One sees two, three, four, and even five year olds chugging away. Contrary to what many people think, that is not the cause of alcoholism. It is more likely to be the cause of an unhealthy capacity to do without close human relationships. That's what happened to Bobby. He came to love himself and his possessions more than he loved other people.

And it has been noticed that some mothers who are breast feeding manage to hold the baby as far away as is physically possible. It looks contorted. The baby's mouth is at the breast while the rest of the tiny body seems to be off in space. Those mothers fear closeness. The reasons are numerous. The most common and most readily overcome reason is that such mothers are afraid of the sexual sensations that accompany nursing. It would help them to know that it is natural. One body next to another arouses sexual sensations in many instances. In the intimacy of nursing, arousal is inevitable because the breast and sex organs function in unison.

Another fear, somewhat less common, is that body boundaries will become blurred. This may occur in mothers who are uncertain about their own boundaries. In the intimacy of holding a baby, uncertainty increases. Is the baby a part of one's body, as was the case before birth, or is he or she a separate person who will become ever more separate in the course of development?

Bobby's first nurse was carefully chosen. She came from one of the better employment agencies and had excellent references.

One of the principal job specifications for nannies in that family's social class was that they speak grammatical English without an accent. That doesn't mean only without a foreign accent. It means without a New York accent. And no Black English. British accents were fine, better than American, provided they were not cockney. Of course, one couldn't expect Oxford English, so one settled for ordinary, fair English. Scottish burrs were acceptable. So the nannies were usually English or Scottish with a good grammar school education. Irish were out. It wasn't a good idea to engage an Irish nanny even if her English was impeccable. For one thing, there would be quarrels with the loyal Brits in the household. Worse still, she might take the child into a Catholic church instead of a proper Episcopalian one. Perhaps worst of all, it wasn't fashionable.

After seven months, Bobby's first nanny heard from her sister in Scotland that the family needed her there, so off she went. It was a matter of family versus job. Bobby was a job. That's a bad time for babies to have someone familiar disappear. There is no good time. Some times are worse than others. At around seven months of age a baby has become accustomed to the principal caregiver. He is beginning to be able to tell one face from another, whereas before that he was only able to distinguish people by feel and smell. He clings to familiar persons and is wary of strangers. This is not a good time for the familiar person to disappear.

Disappearance, in itself, is a problem for a baby who does not know that an out-of-sight person still exists somewhere. It takes many years for a child to learn that a person exists continuously.

Meanwhile out-of-sight is no joke to a baby. It is a traumatic loss. That's why babies cry when mother leaves the room. It doesn't appear serious to adults, who know about continuous existence. To a baby, it feels tragic.

What to do about it? Keep coming back. That's one way babies learn that mother always comes back. Another way is to play the peek-a-boo game. Babies squeal with delight at this because, to them, it is more than a game. It is a lesson in disappearance and return in rapid succession. Babies can play this thousands of times before they get the idea that the face that is gone at one moment is back at the next. The delight is more than ordinary pleasure. It is profound reassurance.

When Bobby's parents were in town, the current nanny presented him to his parents at exactly five-thirty every evening. Needless to say, he was dressed in the latest designer baby clothes and was spanking clean. He had already had his supper and bath, so he smelled good too. He had been put on the toilet and was cleanly diapered and rubberized. If he had a toilet accident or set up a howl, he was snatched out of the room. Nothing unpleasant could be permitted to mar those well-ordered lives. When he got to know his parents, he cried when the time came for him to be removed from the scene. That didn't matter. Guests were coming for cocktails, or his parents were going out.

Bobby grew up with the best physical care and little love. His nannies did their jobs. One or two of them even became fond of him. At bottom, however, he was a job. On the nanny's day off there was always a replacement. The routine was the same regardless of the caregiver. He was fed and dressed in the morning, crawled around and played with his toys when he reached crawling age. Then lunch and to the park in his carriage for his afternoon nap when the weather permitted.

Park time was socializing time for the nannies. The proper British nannies in uniform had their own benches in the park and their own social life. They didn't talk to the black domestics who took care of the middle-class babies from the West Side of the park. They pretended not to understand their English.

As Bobby grew older, the routine changed a bit because of his longer waking hours. The nannies had to play with him some. The one he had when he was fourteen months old—the age when a baby needs to toddle around and explore—was lazy and frightened. It takes some nimble following the child around to keep up with him. That nanny was afraid of being held responsible if he hurt himself, so she kept him as sedentary as she could. Bobby fought it, but he couldn't win.

Of course, he couldn't be kept entirely immobile. He was allowed to use the play equipment in the park if it was in the "right" playground where only the best East Side kids were taken. But it was limited. He wasn't allowed to stray too far. Ideally, a toddler should be free to roam and followed to be sure that he doesn't get lost or injured. The boundaries of Bobby's roaming were restricted by the nanny's laziness.

Of course Bobby had more than enough toys in his room. He didn't get much fun out of playing with them because the nannies wanted them to be arranged neatly. Often, he threw things around. They didn't read his message, which was that he wasn't learning how to play. Then he had to be disciplined, which usually meant sitting still for longer than is tolerable for a child.

Physical development was proceeding normally, so Bobby managed to toddle around despite the restraints. Toddlers have enormous curiosity. They are little explorers who find everything interesting, including themselves. They act as though they have discovered walking, which in a way is true. They crow about it. But walking gives the child maximum pleasure only if there is a gleam in the eye of the beholder. Instead of a gleam, Bobby got disapproval. After *no*, the second word he learned was *dirty*. It seemed that everything interesting was dirty. If Bobby had had the potential to become a scientist, it was squelched early in his life.

The nannies liked to take long walks in the park with their colleagues. They knew one another, often because they had been trained at the same nanny's school in England. Even if they had just met, they were recognizable by their proper uniforms and monogrammed carriages (which were never called *carriages* because that is a lower-class American word for *pram*). For those walks, the children were strapped in their prams and later in their strollers. So the nannies got the exercise. The children got training in sitting still.

They let up somewhat on the sitting still in nursery school because the teachers were well trained in early childhood education. They knew quite a bit more than the nannies. Not until prep school did Bobby get an education in contradiction—sit still in classes, in the dining room, but excel in athletics.

Bobby learned to talk as he listened to the nannies talk. They didn't talk directly to him very often, except to tell him what to do or to scold him. This is not the best way for a child to learn to talk. In fact, they don't learn to talk at all that way in the sense of conversation or communication. They learn only words, language, by overhearing. What they really need is someone to talk *to* them. Most of the talk Bobby heard was *around* him or *at* him.

Bobby learned to speak, but not to communicate. Communication involves some awareness of the other person, of what effect one is having upon the other. By that definition, many adults who can speak do not communicate. He did not get to care enough about other people to want to communicate in that way. He cared a lot about Bobby. No one noticed that until much later in his life.

When Bobby was two, the cook told his parents that the nanny hit the liquor supply while they were out. They fired her. That's another especially bad time in a child's psychological development for someone familiar to disappear. For a while, there was a succession of temporary nannies until a more permanent one could be found.

Bobby was bewildered by this veritable parade of new faces. He screamed when he saw them, which was taken as a sign that he was a difficult baby. The nannies, wanting the job, forced themselves upon him despite his screams.

Bobby turned inward. He had his stuffed animals, his bottle, his thumb, until they tied it down at night. He became dreamy.

Nobody noticed. It was convenient because he was more docile that way.

When he was two and a half, the nursery school interviews began. By then he was a withdrawn child who didn't appear troublesome. With his parents' social connections and his impeccable clothing and behavior, he got into the school of his parents' choice. His education at the right schools was assured. Nursery school and the best elementary school in town, then a good prep school – the one his father had attended. After that, his father's college if his grades were good enough.

The nursery school wouldn't take kids in diapers. That was no problem because Bobby was toilet trained by the time he was a little over a year old. The nanny got a raise for that achievement.

The nanny who toilet trained Bobby won her victory. It is not hard to overpower a child. She was interested in the result, not in what was happening to Bobby inside. She strapped him onto his potty after every meal and waited for him to perform. Sometimes he did. Much of the time he couldn't. After a few sessions like that, he didn't want to. In the end, he had to stop soiling his diapers because he was forced to sit for progressively longer periods after an "accident." Bladder control was more difficult to accomplish because he couldn't stay dry at night at that early age. For practical purposes, though, he was trained before the age of two.

Predictably, he became constipated a bit later on. That was his only way of holding onto that which he believed was his. It was a self-assertion that no one valued. So they got after him with enemas. The message was a confusing one. Control yourself when we say so, but we'll fix it so you will have to lose control.

The nannies who didn't enjoy playing with him seemed to get a bit too excited when they gave him the enemas. No one noticed the excessive pleasure they took in it.

Bobby learned to perform, not only in the bathroom but also in the living room. And, of course, it was important to be clear about the differences between those two kinds of rooms and the different kinds of performances that were acceptable in each. He got to know what kind of behavior would get approval, what would get him snatched out of the room. Nobody had cared when he needed approval for having learned to walk, but now he showed off and enjoyed the response of the audience. He performed for the applause, not because he cared about the other person or because he was developing a worthwhile skill.

His parents were his best audience. He enjoyed his time with them as he began to know how to entertain them. They so admired how he looked and some of the things he did. He learned not to do the "naughty" things. They especially enjoyed him when he began to speak. They valued conversation. And he was clever. It livened up their cocktail hour.

Bobby had a hard time with the other kids in nursery school. He took what he wanted. All kids do at that age, before they have learned a modicum of respect for other people. Bobby didn't learn about other people and their rights. What he did learn was how to be slick. He began to limit his grabbing and hitting to when the teacher wasn't looking.

That became Bobby's life-style. All kids figure out what will work best for them. Because he was smart, Bobby learned the rewards of proper-appearing behavior. He never learned to care about other people for their own sakes, but he knew what would get him somewhere with them. His mother was very beautiful, and when he was old enough to be with her more often, he found her to be very different from the nannies. Flattery always got him somewhere with his mother.

Bobby lived in a strange world, neither in his parents' part of the house nor in the servants' quarters. He was more involved in the daily lives of the servants. They were around more of the time. He witnessed their quarrels, their lovemaking, their card games, their drinking. Some were kind to him, others weren't. The cooks were engaged for their ability to cook, not necessarily because they would be kind to Bobby. He got to know which ones would indulge and pet him and which would chase him out of the kitchen.

For a while there was a cook and driver couple who were fond of Bobby. They gave him the best sense of family life he had ever known. The cook hugged him, gave him good things to snack on. The driver roughhoused with him. He constructed the fantasy that they were his real parents, that he was adopted by the couple who behaved as though they were his parents, that the cook and driver were allowed to work there so that they could be near him. It was a fantasy that saved his psychological life. It couldn't do more than it could do. It saved Bobby from living completely within himself.

So Bobby didn't live entirely alone with his nanny. His life was peopled by maids, cooks, handymen, drivers, stable boys, nursery school teachers, and other children of suitable social status.

This was both good and bad for Bobby. The good is obvious. He had a facsimile of family life some of the time. The bad was that these people didn't remain forever. And there was so much inconsistency. One cook was kind to him; another shooed him away. One butler-driver played with him; the next one snubbed him. He learned early not to trust.

The conversation around the kitchen table at night was on the raw side. Bobby listened from his room. He heard about who was sleeping with whom. It didn't take him long to catch on to the euphemism. Sleeping with someone had nothing to do with sleeping. And since they were all English speaking, Bobby learned the choice Anglo-Saxon words before he could learn them from the kids at school. He used them with his parents' cocktail guests. They were always good for a laugh. He didn't know why they laughed, but of course he liked the fact that they found him so entertaining.

There were also lots of giggles when the nanny bathed Bobby and didn't protect him from the other help who came and went freely while he was undressed. At the age when a child begins to feel embarrassed and wants to cover up, Bobby began to enjoy strutting around in his birthday suit. The women servants loved it. So did he.

One evening, when he was about four years old, he was in-

vited to visit his mother before cocktail time – during her bath.
The visits continued until he went to boarding school. It was their
secret love life. Not overt, of course. They would talk. Then he
was allowed to watch her dress. So they had a lot of time together.
Bobby didn't enjoy it as much as one might expect. It was too
frightening.

Where was his dad? Bobby didn't know, at first, that his parents were divorcing and that Dad had left their home. He was
about five when he found out. His father had liberal visitation
rights, but he rarely exercised them because he was out of town
most of the time.

Bobby's mother began to have a series of lovers. They all tried
to behave as they believed a man should with a boy. What did you
do in school? Who is going to win the pennant? Bobby knew they
weren't interested in him. Just showing off to his mother.

When he was eight years old, his mother remarried. His stepfather had two children, who lived with their mother. They vis-
ited on weekends and for a month in the summer. Sometimes it
was fun. Most of the time it was two against one. They took it out
on Bobby that their father had left them for his mother.

During the summer, Bobby spent a few weeks with his father
and his new family. They had a baby boy. Bobby's stepmother
was devoted to her baby. She was superficially pleasant to
Bobby. She had in mind that her child would have to share his in-
heritance with Bobby. Bobby's father was in his early forties and
in good health, but some people think about those things far in ad-
vance. In her coldness toward him, his stepmother reminded him
of the nannies. Not that he remembered them very well. His
memory was of the chilly emotional climate more than of individuals. He was used to it and had his own ways of dealing with it. The
less he was liked, the more he liked himself.

Bobby spent lots of time at the mirror. A modern day Narcis-
sus. He had watched his mother doing it. He even tried her
makeup once, but he didn't like the way it looked on him. He tried
her clothes too. When he looked at himself in the mirror he was

seized with a desire to masturbate in women's clothing. He had to be careful. There was always a maid prowling around.

When Bobby was too old for a nanny, Martha, a young sleep-in maid was hired to take care of him. His mother was between marriages then and dating quite frequently. Martha was twenty-two and lonely. She lay down with Bobby when she put him to bed. Again, it was a subtle seduction that worked in two ways. It saved him from turning completely inward. The cook-driver couple who were so kind to him had made a start in that direction. That kept Bobby open to human interaction. That saved him from really serious emotional problems that might have rendered him too sick to function in the world.

His contact with Martha had its sexual undertones, of course. Martha didn't intend to be overtly seductive. But Bobby himself became seductive. He was used to parading around naked and didn't stop as he got older. By the time he was eight, ten, twelve, his mother was remarried and busy with her new social life. There was only Martha. He persuaded her to teach him about sex. She was above actual child seduction, but Bobby was clever and talked her into believing it was educational. At first it was a lesson in anatomy. In displaying herself, Martha got turned on. She allowed him to masturbate her. By his early teens, Martha had taught him all he needed to know about how to turn a woman on.

When he got to boarding school, he was ahead of his classmates in that subject. He knew what to do with girls, and they were not unwilling. News of his skill spread through the girls' wing, and Bobby was never lonely again. He didn't have trouble getting them to have intercourse. He discovered quickly that smoking pot enhanced his pleasure. He didn't get to the hard stuff until his senior year. Heroin was out of the question in his social class at that time. Cocaine was just becoming fashionable, and you couldn't beat Bobby when it came to fashion.

He got through college in a fog. Cars, girls, and drugs. By this time he didn't care to visit with either parent. He spent his vacations traveling around Europe with friends. No hitchhiking and vans for him. He had enough money to rent a Mercedes and to stay in the best hotels.

His stepfather did take enough interest to ask Bobby how he could get through college on so much dope. After all, as an Ivy League school, it had its standards. Bobby explained. He majored in philosophy. He knew how to string words together. Nobody knew what he was talking about when he engaged in classroom discussion, but he was a good talker. Even the professor thought his contributions were profound. He didn't make Phi Beta Kappa, but he passed.

After college, the family connections got him a job on Wall Street. The idea was for him to get some experience and then go for an M.B.A. He got lots of experience, but it wasn't in business. He didn't need money, so he showed up on the job when he felt like it, in between ski trips to Switzerland and surfing in California. The firm didn't really need him. They had made a place for him to please his father, so it didn't matter whether he came to work. He could say that he had a job when it suited his purpose to appear to be employed. He had already inherited a small fortune from his grandparents and, of course, was expecting more from his father one day. He could do as he pleased.

What pleased him was women. Not sex. Company. Women were so easy to get. He didn't ever have to be lonely. He hated to pay the price, though. *They* wanted sex. He was a master mechanic, thanks to Martha. It began to bore him, even with pot. With coke he preferred to dance all night. And he kept going through women as though, if he had enough of them, he'd find someone right for him. He didn't realize that the only right person for him was himself.

He began dating less and less frequently. He'd show up at the latest fashionable club alone. Women flocked around him. He was alone in a crowd.

Chapter 9

Narcissism

Bob was an underprivileged child. This may come as a surprise because we are accustomed to equating privilege with wealth. We see the material luxuries and wonder how one can say that such a child is underprivileged. That's the adult's eye view. From the child's point of view, wealth is to be loved. That's privilege. Bobby was an underprivileged child who wore designer clothes and rode in limos. What could he see from a limo? He envied the kids on the buses, who seemed to have more freedom. Kids like to see all there is to see in the world.

Subtle seductions know no economics. They can affect the poor little rich child in the same way as they affect the poor little poor one. There is a difference, of course. Children in wealthy families endure their suffering in more elegant surroundings, with better food and clothing. The food matters because good nutrition is important. Keeping warm matters too. But babies can't read the labels and logos on their clothing, so they don't care about that, nor whether their is home decorated by Sister Parish or the Salvation Army.

There is one important advantage to wealth for children. It makes it possible for parents who are unable to care for their children to turn them over to someone else – with any luck, someone competent. Poor people do that too, of course. The difference here is that, as with everything else, the wealthy can buy the best. They don't always do so, however. Sometimes they buy the most fashionable, which is not necessarily synonymous with best.

A nanny who has chosen her work because she likes children can be a better caregiver than a mother who is unhappy about mothering and prefers doing other things. Poor mothers don't usually have the option, although they sometimes have grandmothers and aunts and such to call upon. There are also arrangements, all too often makeshift, for mothers who have to work. The quality of such arrangements ranges from excellent to terrible.

Day care can be excellent, especially if very young children have one caregiver for no more than three children, and if they are not left for more than six hours. That applies hardly anywhere. Under those conditions, plus a good physical plant, day care has a lot to offer. It helps the child become a social being more quickly and easily. And it gives the mothers a breather so that she can do some adult things for a few hours a day. But it has to be top quality.

Poorly funded day care is likely to be warehouse care, with incompetent and sometimes abusive "caregivers." If more people knew what a difference the first few years of life make, we'd elevate child care to a prestigious profession, provide caregivers with rigorous training, at least as good as we give our M.B.A.s, and pay them more than we pay our generals. The product is people. We can improve the quality of the product in one generation.

It's a myth that poverty causes people to be inadequate parents. Poverty is an evil in its own right, without all the attachments such as that it's a breeder of crime, mental illness, parental neglect and all that. Why not blame it simply because it just plain isn't right for people to want for the necessities of life? Then we'd be in a better position to cure all the other ills by getting at their real causes.

Money (or the lack of it) also doesn't determine whether people can love their children. If we had to be rich to be able to love, the world would be in worse shape than it already is. There are rejected children, rich and poor. There are also loved children, rich and poor. Poor parents who are coping with the problem of daily survival don't always have to burden the children with their worries.

There was a play, *I Remember Mama*, about a family during the Great Depression. In it, Mama kept telling the kids that, if the family ran short of money, they'd have to tap the family bank account. The kids didn't know until they had grown up that there had never been a bank account. Mama protected them from adult worries.

It's a not-so-subtle seduction to pile worries onto children who can't do anything about them but feel helpless and frightened. The seductive aspect is that the adult is asking the child to take on adult responsibilities. Children, by and large, cannot become breadwinners. So what can they do, share the worry? How does that help?

Probably in very dire poverty, it's not easy to spare the child. If they are hungry, they know it. And it's hard for parents to conceal abject despair.

The affliction that we call *narcissism*—excessive self-love—results from the absence of love from others. It affects rich and poor alike. When there are problems, including physical illness, the rich have it better. They can have doctors, nurses, housekeepers, comfortable hospitals. But money and good judgment don't always go together, which is why money doesn't always buy the best. The most fashionable doctors are not always the best at doctoring. Some are, of course. Some are more skilled at making social contacts. When Gloria Vanderbilt, the poor little rich girl, was having nightmares, they called in about fifty doctors. Not one of them realized that the child was being pulled apart, used, se-

duced by the adults in her life. To be fair to all professions, the
judge at her custody hearing didn't catch on either.

While the very poor worry about their daily bread, the very
rich, like Bobby's parents, worry about their social status. The
middle class, many of whom have arrived there by upward mobil-
ity, want their children to maintain that status, or even go a notch
higher. So middle-class parents worry about getting their children into good schools. The very rich don't have to worry about
that because the schools know where their contributions come
from. The poor make do with the public schools, good or bad.

Babies, no matter how well nourished, get sick and die unless
they have human contact in addition to nourishment. Dr. René
Spitz discovered this sad fact when he was called in as a con-
sultant by an institution that was providing excellent physical
care on an assembly-line basis. The babies perished from absence
of emotional nourishment.

Bobby got something more than those institutionalized babies. He had one nanny at a time all to himself. Whoever she was,
she had to provide some human contact during feeding, bathing,
diapering. Otherwise, Bobby would have turned out to be much
more emotionally disturbed than he was, if he had survived at all.

Also, he was displayed to his parents, who held him when
they were assured that he was adequately diapered and rubberized. So we assume he got enough "human touch" to survive. Not
quite enough to enable him to feel good enough about himself, to
enable him to love others. It isn't true that altruistic love is the
best kind. We have to have some for ourselves to be able to spare
some for other people.

Egotistical, self-centered, narcissistic – all mean more or less
the same thing. They sound pejorative. We can hardly keep ourselves from disliking such people. But we might feel a little
kindlier toward them if we understand how they got that way.

A person in Bobby's plight doesn't simply stew in dry psychological juices. If a good solution to an unbearable situation is not
at hand, the person contrives the best one possible under the cir-

cumstances. Bobby's best solution under his circumstances was to turn to himself. A narcissist tries to be his own best friend. It doesn't work because he is looking for love where it isn't. So it's not a good choice, merely the only one available.

Narcissists appear as though they have "too much ego" when, in fact, they have very low self-esteem, for which they are compensating. Knowing this helps us to understand them. It doesn't always make them more likeable. Not all of them succeed in polishing it up with charm, as Bob was able to do. When they are not even charming, they are unpleasant to be with. By the age of three, Bobby was that way. He was boisterous, grabby, walked all over the other children in nursery school. When thwarted, he became sullen and withdrawn. Later, he learned to accomplish the same purpose with sophistication, charm, and polish.

To the credit of his nursery school teachers, they worried about him. Unfortunately, there was not much they could do about it because they had little access to the parents, who would not have accepted their advice anyway.

What Bobby needed was therapy. At that early age? Yes— that's when a large slice of the problem could have been corrected. Probably nothing would have made up for the deficits of the first few months. That's when damage can become irreversible—which is too bad because it is so easily averted. All one has to do in those early months is "relate" to the baby. The baby will do the rest. He will respond and proceed in his development. It doesn't take much, and it's worth it. You get a large return on a small investment.

For Bobby, the first few months went down the drain. What was lost was an initial good feeling, a feeling that life is pleasant, confident expectation that all will go well, trust, love. Also lost were such things as enhanced intellectual capacity. Intellect is like a muscle. It needs exercise from the beginning.

Sharpening a baby's mind is one of the appropriate seductions. The mothering person (fathers can do it too) "seduces" the baby's mind to make it work. This does not mean teaching the baby math. It means whetting his interest in the goings-on around him. The most interesting thing to a baby is a person babbling to him.

The series of nannies was terrible for Bobby. An infant or young child in favorable circumstances gets used to having the same, consistent person around every minute of every day. At first it is the way she holds him that becomes familiar – her touch, her smell, her voice, even her footsteps. To be treated in a predictable way every time one is fed, changed, bathed, and to be cooed at in a familiar voice lays the groundwork for a sense of security that lasts a lifetime.

After a few weeks of this, the baby smiles. Everyone who has been near a baby knows that. It is useful to know why it happens and what is happening to the baby to bring it about.

What is happening is phenomenal. The baby becomes familiar with the friendly face peering at him over the crib. He notes that there is a configuration to it – two eyes, a nose, and a mouth. If the face has brought pleasure and relief from hunger, the baby remembers and makes a connection between the pleasure and relief that accompanies the arrival of the face, so he smiles at it. It has been shown that babies will smile only at a full face in motion, not at a still face or at a profile.

The baby does not, at first, distinguish one face from another. She will smile at a Halloween mask. This may make mothers, and especially grandmothers, unhappy. But that's their problem. The baby is doing fine. Imagine! In a few short weeks the baby has used memory, anticipation, volition, recognition and has combined all these complex matters into a pattern that begins to make her responsive to other persons. The baby becomes a human being. Animals don't smile.

But, it might be argued, if one face was the same as another, what difference did it make to Bobby that the faces changed so frequently?

It made an enormous difference. The smile is the culmination of all that went before. So we go not just by the smile, but also by what the experience leading up to the first smile was like. And the smile is only the beginning. The baby still needs the same, consistent person to keep him going on to the next step in his development. He cannot do it with constantly changing faces. If they don't keep changing, he will soon become able to differentiate between a familiar person and a stranger.

Did Bobby smile at the appropriate developmental time? Very likely. A baby who does not reach the "smiling response" is usually in even greater trouble than Bobby was. Failure to reach this developmental milestone might be neurological. Don't wait too long to get it checked out. There is often grave danger in thinking that babies will outgrow problems. They only outgrow the ones that appear to be problems but aren't. That's why it is so important to know what behavior is appropriate to what age. What Grandma thinks is a problem may be normal behavior to an expert. And what you hope will be outgrown may be something you shouldn't wait about. Sometimes it's worth a consultation to find out. Don't ask your pediatrician unless she really knows. Ask a psychoanalytically trained therapist.

Let's take a simple example of when to worry and when to remain calm. Fear of strangers is not a problem in the second half of the first year of life. It's a problem if it *doesn't* happen. This is when the child begins to be able to distinguish the familiar face from that of a stranger.

Bobby had good endowment, so he reached these important psychological landmarks despite the fact that encouragement from those who should have helped him was on the meager side. Most of the job of development is up to the child. Human infants, if they are normally endowed, come into the world equipped to make the most of what awaits them. Parents have only to provide favorable conditions.

This should come as a great relief. For much too long, psychology has put the emphasis on what the parent does. Our latest information, however, is that much is up to the child. Of course, this applies only if the experiences that are provided are within decent limits. The child cannot conquer every circumstance.

So Bobby managed to smile without much help, but he couldn't get past it very successfully. After a few months, when a normally developing child becomes discriminating, Bobby continued to smile at strangers.

There was a play in the London theatre many years ago, one of those farces that London theatre is famous for, entitled *The Dutchess Who Smiled at Everyone.* That kind of "skill" makes for good social butterflies and good politicians. It doesn't make for the ability to love special people. Once in a while there's a news item about a rock star throwing a party for two thousand friends. How can anyone have two thousand friends?

To have become choosy about whom to smile at, Bobby would have to have had one or two special people in his life from the beginning. Normally, a baby begins to be able to discriminate by about five, six, seven months of age. Family faces become familiar. Everyone else is a stranger. Parents worry. Their formerly friendly and outgoing baby cries when someone comes to visit. People explain to baby, "It's your Aunt Susie." If Aunt Susie hasn't been around much, it could be the woman in the moon.

Don't get panicky if "stranger anxiety" appears not to be happening. Some babies don't show it. Your baby may not be a dramatist, in which case it can pass unnoticed unless you watch for it very closely. Sometimes it only shows when the baby becomes curious about strangers. Babies are inquisitive, in a hurry to learn about the world. They can become so absorbed with the discovery of someone's eyeglasses or necklace that they forget to be frightened.

Don't apologize to the "stranger" if the baby cries or turns away, and don't force the baby to accept her even if she is Grandma. Blood isn't thicker than water to a baby.

It didn't help Bobby to have to confront strange faces every day—not only new nannies, but cooks, housemaids, the parents' guests. It must have seemed like at least two thousand people to him. He screamed a lot. His parents wanted Bobby to display social graces to their guests. After all, he had been smiling so charmingly a short while before. The nannies worried that they'd be dismissed because they couldn't get Bobby to behave "properly." Nobody took the baby's feelings into account. They all felt annoyed and rejected. Everyone got mad at poor little Bobby.

Disapproval rubbed off on him. He couldn't miss that he wasn't pleasing anyone. He acquired a disapproved-of self-image. No one can live comfortably with that. That's why he turned to himself for approval, comfort, love. He couldn't find it, because it wasn't there. It works like a bank. You can't withdraw what hasn't been deposited.

When he was old enough, he looked elsewhere. He imagined women would have it for him. That's inevitably disappointing because we can never capture at age thirty what was needed at age three months. The time is past. Of course, we have all encountered people who try.

Why doesn't it work? Why can't one make up belatedly for what was missed? After a baby suckles at the breast for the better part of a year, after he is cooed at and played with and tossed and cuddled, he is ready to move on to other things. It's not unheard of for an adult, man or woman, to try to get cuddling from another person. And it's good if it isn't the only thing that matters in life. When it is needed too desperately, it never comes to an end, except a dead end. A child moves on, becomes interested in walking, investigating, learning to talk, to play. Adults who are still at the breast do not become the explorers and venturers in this world. Too late is too late.

A child begins to speak at about eighteen months of age, give or take a little to account for individual differences. We take speech so for granted that we don't realize what an accomplishment it is. It means, among other things, that the mind has developed. The baby now has what psychologists call a *representational world*. A word is a symbol for something, not the thing itself. The word *Mommy* stands for a very important person *and* for all the complex feelings surrounding her image.

We use words to communicate. Before acquiring the ability to speak, the child comes to expect to be understood without words. Grunts, gestures, crying usually get him what he wants. Now the wants become more complex. The child gradually begins to realize that other persons, including mother, cannot read his mind the way mother seemed to do when he was a baby. He has to talk to her. Grunting and gesturing no longer get him what he wants. He has to say *cookie* in order to get one.

There's more to it. It isn't simply that talking gets the baby what he wants. In the best of circumstances there is a dawning awareness of the other person as someone who needs to be communicated with. This includes caring about whether one is getting across, caring about the receiver of the communication.

Bobby learned to speak eloquently, largely because he was bright. He used speech to get what he wanted, but it didn't include the total accomplishment of this complex developmental achievement. He didn't come to care about others. He learned how to appear to care, to deceive. That's what got him through college without getting him an education. That's what made it easy for him to sweet talk women.

He didn't love enough to communicate in the full sense of the word. Normal people have a certain amount of love in storage that makes it possible to care whether the person to whom they wish to communicate are receiving their messages.

The word *no* becomes a favorite of the child just learning to speak. It comes on the heels of that wonderful time of life when the child is an elated explorer. He is interested in everything. People say no to him thousands of times. He can't lick them so he joins them. He begins to say no to everything. Ask him whether he wants a cookie and he will say no—which has nothing to do with the fact that he will accept one happily.

It's an exercise. Children overwork it until they become really convinced that they own it. *No* says, "I'm becoming a person in my own right, with a person's right of refusal." Understood that way, perhaps we can see it as something besides "the terrible twos." It would be terrible if it *didn't* happen.

Just when you think it will never happen comes the blessed day when the child has made his point and can begin to say yes. The charming, smiling toddler of former days is back!

Bobby never learned to say yes. He learned the word, and he used it when it served its purpose for him. It never represented true agreement with another person. He never came to like other people enough to want to agree with them. He did learn how to appear to be agreeable when it could get him somewhere.

As Bobby grew older, more problems were added to the earlier ones. The cumulative effect was building. Bobby realized more and more how his needs collided with those of the adults, not only his parents but the bewildering array of strangers who served the household.

The servants could be quite coarse among themselves. They believed the myth that children are too young to understand, so Bobby's presence didn't stop them. The women who giggled over his nudity seduced him into exhibiting himself. Most children, by the age of four, five, six, become modest about their bodies and seek cover. Not Bobby. He lapped up their voyeurism, when another child might have protested. And he used their four-letter words to entertain his parents and their guests.

Was that a seduction? Yes. He was being used for their entertainment. Bobby sensed that, but he was willing to play the game because he needed every bit of recognition he could get. That his parents misused him was probably worse than that the servants did. He knew where the authority lay.

Bobby himself was fascinated with his body, especially his penis, of course. That's fine. Children need to be proud of their bodies. Bobby could have benefited from moderate admiration. That's the fine line between just enough seduction and too much. Children need to feel good about their bodies, and a little admiration will help that feeling along. Bobby got too much.

It taught him that adults like to look. Of course they do, in moderation, as a prelude to sex perhaps. But to involve a child in that is too seductive. The child becomes caught up in it and, as in Bobby's case, enjoys it so much that it keeps him from moving on to better forms of sexual enjoyment. The women in Bob's adult life didn't mind admiring his body, up to a point. They didn't appreciate it as the be all and end all.

Then there was Bobby's toilet training. He had to be clean and well controlled, no matter what it did to him. Many children are trained like that. As adults, they swoon over a mess. It doesn't even have to be dirt. Drop a newspaper on the floor and it becomes unbearable. The feelings of the offender don't matter. The floor has to be clean at all costs. Psychologists call that a compulsion. Things have to be clean and neat lest the unbearable anxiety break out.

On the other extreme are people whose toilet training was overpermissive and thus they are still messing. Those are the ones who throw the newspaper on the floor. Put those two types together and you have a bad marriage.

A third, more rugged character is in perpetual rebellion against toilet training. Those types make deliberate messes just to prove that no one can boss them around. We might say of these people who had toilet-training trouble as young children that they never got out of the bathroom, psychologically speaking.

A common form of "remaining in the bathroom" is bathroom humor. Bobby's parents enjoyed bathroom jokes in the living room. That's a lot better than getting the two rooms mixed up. Adults who are so far gone that they actually perform bathroom functions outside the bathroom have to be hospitalized.

Two-year-olds are fascinated with toilet functions. Adults are supposed to be over it. They shouldn't have to talk about it anymore, except to their physicians when something goes wrong. But many people can't get it off their minds.

What was seductive about Bobby's participation in bathroom humor? Adults are supposed to exercise leadership, teach children how to grow up—if they know. Good nursery school teachers know how to steer these childish interests into socially acceptable channels. They make provisions for water play, which, rather than curbing the child's interest in urination, allows him to play it out to his heart's content and get it out of his system. The other nursery school devices, like clay and finger paint, serve the same purpose. They teach controlled messiness instead of forbidding it altogether.

Such activities allow children to get past toilet interests in their own sweet time so that they don't remain fascinated with it forever or, worse still, so that they don't get the idea that it's wrong or bad. Messing with clay has the added advantage of turning the natural need to mess into something creative. That's the ideal way of helping children get over "life in the bathroom." If they are allowed to play it out, they'll get over it in due time because other things become more interesting.

First Bobby was toilet trained. Then, when his self-control became too much of a good thing, he became constipated. The enemas began. No one realized that his withholding was a form of self-assertion. Of course, it is not healthy in the long run, but it should have been read as a message. The message is similar to the *no*—I will do as I please, not what you demand of me.

He became utterly confused. First, control yourself. Now, perform on demand. When he held back in order to retain what he perceived to be his, it was forced out of him with enemas that made him lose the control he had been taught to maintain.

Enemas make children feel invaded, helpless, angry. A child should be given an enema by prescription only. Even then, physicians don't always take the psychological consequences into account. A child needs an enema when the constipation is life threatening and can't be treated any other way.

Bobby's nannies were not competent to decide that. For one thing, they enjoyed giving the enemas. Many a child has had them overdone because the adult takes secret pleasure in doing it. Not that the adult is aware of this. One has to observe very closely to notice the zeal. The child notices.

Enemas also provide a terrible feeling of being overpowered.

Bobby had the usual inoculations that children have to have. Although children don't like the injections, they know that it is not done with enjoyment, for the other person's pleasure. Then it feels different from being overpowered by something in which the adult is taking such obvious pleasure. Obvious to the child, that is. The person who is doing it is wholly unconscious of the enjoyment; it is all rationalized as a hygienic necessity.

The number of people who linger, psychologically, in the bathroom cannot be counted, although psychoanalysts see them every day and find it to be a form of sexual pleasure that uses the wrong organs of the body. It keeps people from full enjoyment of sex with the organs that are designed for that purpose. That's why sex therapy that consists of instruction in the mechanics of sex cannot be as helpful as it promises. It doesn't get at the unconscious causes of the sexual dysfunction. Unconscious fascination with toilet functions is not the only cause of sexual dysfunction. It's a powerful and very common one.

When Bobby's parents split up, no one thought it important to tell him about it. His father simply disappeared. There was no one Bobby could ask. Children know when their questions are unwelcome. So if there had been the slightest chance that his father could have become a meaningful, real person to Bobby, that chance was averted. Bobby did what children do. He created a fantasy of a perfect father who was just like him. But the fantasy didn't help him learn how to get along with real, live men. He couldn't tolerate their flaws, the major one of which was that they could leave him. Bob never had any men friends.

Women were different. Bobby's mother used him to fill her loneliness before she started dating again. Not that she ever had any real time for him. Her bath and dressing times were the times for entertaining Bobby. He was "entertained" beyond what a little boy can endure.

A boy has to do something to contain the excitement of having a nude adult woman all to himself. It's too hot to handle, regardless of who the woman is, but it's hottest when it's his mother.

Each child creates a unique solution that very quickly becomes unconscious, surfacing only when the child tells his therapist about it. If the child doesn't have a therapist until he's an adult, it still comes out those many years later.

Bobby created a fantasy to handle the excitement, which was what many boys in that circumstance do, with individual variations. He *became* his mother in his unconscious. He became a female in order not to be excited by one. These kinds of "solutions" don't work. They are attempts that fail because they make more trouble rather than less. But they are all that a child can do. Those who do not succeed in containing the excitement, even in such distorted ways, find it unbearable. Then the problem is likely to emerge in the form of symptoms such as nightmares, bedwetting, learning disorders, hyperactivity.

Bobby handled his unbearable feelings by becoming his mother in his unconscious fantasy. It couldn't work because the very solution became another problem. Now he had to deal with the thought that, if he is a woman, what becomes of his treasured penis!

Yes, we are now discussing that much misunderstood matter of *castration anxiety*. A boy and man will do anything to get rid of that terrible feeling. What Bobby did was masturbate while wearing his mother's clothing. That assured him that his penis was still there. Since he was his mother as well as himself in his fantasy, it also allowed him to fantasize that his mother had a penis. The idea there is to assert that there is no such thing as castration. It doesn't convince.

When Bobby's mother began dating and ultimately remarried, Bobby was again relegated to the smallest part of her life. He went from too high to too low. It didn't help his self-esteem to be on this sort of roller coaster. It didn't help him to trust people either. What it did was push him further into himself. He didn't become noticeably withdrawn, as some children might have. He became withdrawn with a facade of outgoingness. His insincerity was hard to detect. Even Bob wasn't always aware of it.

It wasn't hard for teenage Bobby to con Martha. He was already adept at conning people. What's wrong with introduction to sex by a maid? It used to be the tradition in the "best" households in Europe, probably still is. Can that account for the philandering husbands that those upper-class Europeans become? Nothing is quite that simple. We'd have to take individual life histories into account. Clearly, however, it is a factor.

This brings us to the generation gap. Teenagers speak of it negatively. They're negative about so many things that one more doesn't seem to matter. Don't pay too much attention to their words. The generation gap serves a very useful purpose. Children never say so, but they love it. They feel unprotected without it. You'll never know that from what they say.

Teenagers have the most creative arguments for breaching the gap. Especially now that teenage sex is so prevalent, the arguments go, "You know that we are doing it, so what's wrong with having my girlfriend sleep with me at home?" Or, "It's so hypocritical of you to pretend it isn't happening." They'll tell you how stupidly inconsistent you are. Old fashioned. Not with it. Hiding behind standards that you yourself do not adhere to. Why can you do it and not I? You don't accept my sexuality. It's like the nineteenth century around here.

Don't let yourself be talked out of your position by these Philadelphia lawyers. The best thing you can do for them is hold your ground. You don't even have to be right all the time. Nobody can be. It's more important to be firm and consistent, as long as you are not altogether unreasonable.

Life with an adolescent isn't easy. The English psychoanalyst, D. W. Winnicott, said that the only cure for adolescence is five years. He was wrong. It's more like ten.

Teenagers are going through one more round of the Oedipus complex and of anxiety about becoming adults. They want to be grown up, independent. It's an in-between stage of life, when wishes to be an adult clash with the residual feelings of being a child.

The adolescent's challenge does not really get to the heart of the matter. He isn't really asking whether you will allow him to have sex with his girlfriend in your house. That's only the way he has to put it. An unconscious question lies beneath the conscious one.

The hidden question is designed to test whether you will uphold the incest taboo. The girlfriend is merely a surrogate. The real question is, "Now that I am physically capable of fulfilling my incestuous wishes, will you allow it?" It's all unconscious, so don't ask him about it. It is best left unconscious. Much harm can be done by bringing it into the open, except in the course of very carefully conducted therapy.

Sex under the parental roof appears to the child as a frightening breach of the generation gap. This applies equally to boys and girls. The fact is that teenagers are still children in adult bodies. They need parental firmness to help them contain their anxiety. They'll never admit it.

What makes them anxious? Unconscious wishes, which are way ahead of their psychological ability to deal with them. We can look upon these wishes as something they want until they are likely to get it. Then they are scared out of their minds. That's anxiety.

About marriage the Bible says, for this cause shall you leave father and mother and cling to your spouse. What cause? Sex, of course. Were it not for sex, no one would leave father and mother to cling to a stranger who doesn't even cook as well as mother. We have to make it possible for kids to grow up and leave, much as we hate to see them go. If one can have sex at home, why leave?

Eventually, of course, they do leave. But physical departure does not always connote psychological readiness to leave behind childhood wishes and expectations. Many young adults leave home, taking unfinished business with them. It is that business that so often impairs adult relationships. For example, the philandering husband (or wife) may be an overage adolescent still testing whether someone cares enough to stop him. Bob's unfinished business appeared like that, but it was, in fact, that he was unable to stick it out with one person after he detected that she had a human flaw. It is usually not possible to understand behavior by superficial examination. So many similar-appearing actions are caused by different underlying reasons.

Sex with Martha added to Bobby's anxiety. It occurred many years after his visits with his mother in the bath. By now we are familiar with the way these experiences build one upon the other like layers of bricks, or threads in a tapestry.

In a way, boarding school was a relief for Bobby. At least the stimulation there came from contemporaries. It honed Bobby's persuasive skills. The girls fell like flies. It was too easy.

It didn't take long for sex to begin to lose its charge. Bob began to use drugs to give it a boost. A high, whether on alcohol or another drug, promises a quick solution to the pervasive feeling of imperfection that people like Bobby carry within themselves. For life's imperfections to be tolerable, one should have had a very brief illusion of perfection in infancy. That comes from feeling at one–united with a wonderful, all-powerful person. It provides a foundation for everlasting self-esteem.

This doesn't mean that the mothering person has to be perfect in reality. The infant takes care of the discrepancy between the way he needs her to appear and the way she really is by placing outside this cozy little unit of self and mother anything that impairs the perfect feeling.

But this arrangement must not last too long. If it is too prolonged, the individual will never become able to deal with harsh reality. For Bobby, it was the opposite. He didn't have that necessary, although temporary, illusion of perfection. The foundation of self-esteem was not built.

That's where drugs come in. Those who use them describe the high that resembles the perfect union of mother and infant. Those who have been deprived of it at the appropriate time seek it forever after. Too bad it cannot be found.

So Bob never found what he was looking for. First he had

looked for love within himself, where it could not have been. Then his father, mother, nannies – everyone – disappointed him. Then he looked for an alter ego in women, but they were themselves, not Bob. Finally, alcohol and drugs seemed to hold promise. We all know what they really promise – an early demise.

With all those strikes against him, what saved Bobby from greater psychological disaster? A taste of goodness, given to him by the cook-driver couple who were so kind to him. It was not nearly enough to counteract all the rest, but it was something to draw on, money in the bank when his therapist tried to establish rapport with him. Therapy is of avail when the patient has something good from the past that the therapist can connect with, such as the experience of a loving human relationship. Without that, therapy is rough going.

Narcissists are the most difficult for the therapist to connect with because a narcissist's relationship is with himself. Not with his real self. With a fantasy perfect self that no real person can match. Tough competition for a therapist. The person has to be willing to give up the perfect relationship for the sake of engaging in one with a real person. A real person has flaws, which is exactly what the narcissist wants to avoid. In effect, the door is closed. The wedge in Bob's door was that he had had that taste of something good from outside himself. That gave the therapist a chance, a slim one to be sure, to get a foot in Bobby's door.

If Bobby had received therapy at age three, he might have been able to catch up with his psychological development in those areas that were still reparable. The earlier a child is stressed, the more irreversible the damage. Even minutes count. Obstetrical practice is smarter than it used to be. Now babies are given to their mothers immediately after birth. There is no time to lose in helping babies establish human relationships.

Much could have been done for Bobby, even belatedly. In a therapeutic relationship with a skilled child therapist, he would have acquired self-esteem through experiencing the good feelings that can come from human interaction. This would have kept him from the solution to which he had to resort—seeking emotional supplies from within himself by withdrawal into himself. He would have become less egotistical, less self-centered, less narcissistic.

Therapy would have helped Bobby, not only at age three (or earlier), but any time after that. It would have been easier, quicker, and more effective at an early age, however.

Bobby's parents would have been appalled by such a recommendation, even if they had been available to receive it. Some parents don't like to be told that their child needs therapy because they think it reflects on them. More than one parent has kept a child from it with the lopsided reasoning that if the child is in therapy, it means that the parent has a problem! As though the problem goes away if the child is not in therapy. Does appendicitis go away if you don't take the child to a doctor?

Who else besides the nursery school teacher was aware that Bobby needed help? What about the pediatrician? A pediatrician is a physician trained in the medical care of children. Medical training is so complex these days that there is little room for psychoanalytic training as well. Those who seek psychological advice from their children's pediatricians may get a bit of help in small matters. For problems as severe as Bobby's, however, a referral to a psychoanalytically trained child therapist is in order.

Despite their limited training in psychology, pediatricians are asked a great many psychological questions—about weaning, toilet training, thumb sucking, sibling rivalry, sleep problems, tantrums. Some have a feel for the psychological implications; others do not. Some make up answers by the seats of their pants or skirts because people put a great burden on physicians by expecting them to know everything. Others acknowledge that they don't know the answers.

Physicians know that there is such a thing as psychiatry because it is a medical specialty. Don't get psychiatry confused with psychoanalysis, however. Psychiatrists are trained by spending their three-year residencies in mental hospitals, where they learn *psychopharmacology*—administration of medication. Medications are exceedingly useful for controlling the extreme behavior of psychotics, relieving the misery of depression, the horror of intense anxiety. Like aspirin, they relieve symptoms. And also like aspirin, they do not cure.

The better psychiatric residencies offer some training in psychoanalytic psychotherapy in addition to psychopharmacology. And some psychiatric residents go on for psychoanalytic training after or during their residencies. That puts them on a par with those who have had similar psychoanalytic training.

Too bad Bobby couldn't get that kind of help, despite the fact that he lived in a city where such therapists are available. Unfortunately, they are not everywhere. And here is another instance in which a child from a wealthy family has a distinct advantage. Good therapy is expensive. Poor people have to go to clinics, if there are any in their neighborhoods. There used to be an ad about a beverage that was sold "only in the best neighborhoods." The advice was that if it's not sold in your neighborhood, move to a better one. Clever, but not very practical. Therapists tend to cluster in cities. If you live in a small community, you don't have to move, but you might have to travel.

Some mental health clinics provide very good psychotherapy. One has to strike it lucky. Their bad feature is that they are used for training, so a patient might be assigned to an inexperienced therapist who leaves when she has completed her training. The patient is then transferred to another therapist, possibly precisely when what he needs is consistency. A person like Bob, who has had a series of nannies, housekeepers, foster parents, or whatever, doesn't need a series of therapists as well.

On the other hand, a patient can get a great deal of enthusiastic devotion with a less experienced therapist. A more experienced therapist is likely to arrive at a poor prognosis more quickly. Optimism has its advantage. An unfavorable-appearing situation can improve markedly with a therapist who conveys hopefulness and sticks it out.

Chapter 10

Made for Each Other

Alice grew up in a large working-class family. She was the third child, two boys older than she and five children younger. Her household duties began early. She was more mother than sister to the younger children.

The psychological climate was murky. Messages were mixed. The family was superficially religious, attended church regularly, but broke many of the rules.

When the extended family got together, the adults engaged in childish sexually suggestive behavior. The men got drunk and loose. They grabbed at the women and made lewd remarks. Some of the uncles grabbed at the teenage girls. All in fun.

There's nothing wrong with childish sex when practiced by children. When the grownups appear to have remained childish, however, the children are confused. How are they to know what it means to be grown up when there is no one to provide an example? Is that what it's like to be an adult—toilet jokes and sexy jokes and grabbing at everyone indiscriminately?

Alice's father drank a bit more than moderately, not only at family dinners. Every day. Especially when he was laid off at the factory. We know what that does to a man – worry about feeding his large family, assault to his masculinity, idleness. The children were frightened when their father was drunk. He became unruly, sometimes downright nasty. It wasn't great for their mother either. He'd get rough with the kids and violent with her. He was not a truly vicious man. He was mixed up and unable to handle his frustration.

We are overcoming the myth that abused women like it. They endure it because there's no place to go, and for the important psychological reason that people will put up with a great deal in order to have somebody. Children, too, endure whatever they get because they have no other place to go. They become attached to their parents, even mean ones. Some of our courts are beginning to recognize that. It's simpleminded thinking to yank a child out of a home because it appears that the child is being mistreated. We have to take into account that ties have become established that can't be broken without breaking their hearts as well. Good judges are beginning to understand that it is better to help the parents with their problems when that is possible. Sometimes it isn't.

Alice's family lived in a rambling old house with too few rooms for so many children. The two oldest boys slept in the same bed. A younger brother was added to their room when he was old enough to yield the crib to the next baby. Alice slept alone until one of the little sisters, in her turn, was moved out of the permanently occupied crib. Then she and Alice doubled up. In time, two more sisters came to share the room. There would have been no room for the two youngest if it weren't for the fact that, by the time they came along, the two oldest boys were gone. A factory worker's family is not like a farm family in which all hands are needed. Alice's parents were glad the children were growing up and getting out on their own.

The cramped living quarters left no room for privacy. Alice

was aware of her parents' and brothers' bodies, bathing and toileting, sex and fighting.

She wasn't very old when she became a living exhibit for her brothers' curiosity about female anatomy. They would take her into their room, put a chair against the door, and explore her genitals. They liked to show theirs too. There's nothing terribly wrong with that. It happens in every family and it's not so bad when it happens among children. At least it doesn't breach the generation gap.

It did, however, give Alice a lopsided impression about herself in relation to the boys. Not so much a sense of anatomical inferiority. That was there, of course. Some people don't like the idea of penis envy. They think Freud made it up. But all one has to do is follow the current research. Long after Freud presented that idea, it was proven correct by the research in child development carried out by the ego psychologists. It is not difficult to note that it does appear to very young children that boys have something more than girls do. Most people correct that impression later. For some, it lingers because it connects with similar feelings of being deprived, of having less than others.

The main thing, though, was that Alice felt used by two boys who were bigger than she. In her fantasy, that put her in a position similar to mother's. The fantasy had it that she and her mother were overpowered by males. They threw their weight around. She felt she was no match for them. That initiated Alice's life-style—weak, intimidated, helpless, but aroused by being overpowered.

Mother couldn't help. There was no talk about that to correct Alice's false impressions. Not that mother didn't talk to Alice. In fact, Alice was her confidant as they worked together in the kitchen. But that was a one-way street. It was all about Mother's troubles.

Alice's mother was perpetually pregnant. She had varicose veins and found it hard to get around. Yet she had to feed her large and growing-larger family. She knew the kids were playing in the boys' room. It was a respite for her. She didn't have the energy to barge in and initiate another game, a less loaded one, as a more sophisticated mother with more leisure might.

They were all afraid of their father's temper, especially when he had been drinking. Even when he wasn't working, he didn't stay at home during the day. He'd go out to look for work, end up at the bar with his cronies, come home for supper, and roar at everyone. Anything would tick him off. They treaded carefully and tried to stay out of reach.

Life was lived in the kitchen during and after supper. The kids did their homework while Mother and Alice did the dishes. Father drank more beer. He'd already had some before he came home for supper. As he became drunker, he became more irritable. He'd swat whoever was within reach.

Alice discovered early that life is exhausting for women. Marriage looked grim. A number of events got jumbled together in Alice's mind. It didn't seem different whether her mother was attacked in the kitchen or in bed. To Alice, Mother bled in both locations. Blood ran almost like water in that household, especially when the babies were delivered at home. Women's bodies seemed distorted. Alice got used to Mother's swollen belly and swollen legs.

Alice lived in the thick of everything. She learned about boys, babies, sex, bleeding, fighting, all muddled together. Did she learn about love?

That's a hard one. Love wasn't entirely absent in Alice's home, as it was in Bob's. Love is how you define it. For Alice there was an intact family, even an extended family. Everyone lived nearby – grandparents, aunts, uncles, cousins. Being a member of the family meant belonging. That's a big plus. On the other hand, it didn't provide Alice with a feeling of being special. Nobody noticed anything unique about her. Like Eleanor, she was one of the crowd.

Her specialness came from being the oldest girl. She had the privilege of tending the babies, setting the table, helping with cooking and laundry, doing the dishes, taking the kids to school, cleaning house on Saturdays, nursing the kids when they were sick. When the boys went out to play ball after school, Alice peeled potatoes for supper. It doesn't sound great, and it wasn't. But it did give Alice a definite place. She knew where she belonged. That's better than being suspended in space, as Bob was.

Her position in the family also gave her a special closeness to mother. Are we still talking about love? In a way, yes. Alice needed love so much that she milked whatever she got that bore the faintest resemblance to it. And for her mother, the question wasn't simply, did she or didn't she. Mother was tired, wasn't having a great life herself, hadn't had one when she was a child. She did her duty. How can we answer the question of whether that is love? She didn't gush, but she didn't take off and leave the kids. Love is how you find it.

Some ingredients for love were there. Alice had so much time with her mother. They didn't talk intimately. That wasn't Mother's style. Alice made the most of it. She had Mother to herself more often than the others did. It made up for a lot. Many a child would gladly peel potatoes if it would get her special time with Mother. That's all the time Mother had. Compared with Bob's mother, who had only her bath time, it wasn't so bad.

They talked about Mother's pains, about her money worries, about the doings in the aunts' and uncles' families. They never talked about sex directly. Mother would have slapped Alice if she had asked frank questions. Alice knew that. She put two and two together out of her observations. Sometimes it added up to six.

Why would Alice have had to ask about sex when she already knew so much? One reason is that she needed to have her distortions corrected. Another reason, related to that, was to hear from mother that it is good, loving, pleasurable. Alice's mother could not have told her that. What she overheard when one or the other of the aunts came to visit is that life is hard, sex is to be endured, money is always short, men are unfeeling at best and brutal at worst. Pregnancy is painful at both ends and in the middle—painful to conceive, to carry, to deliver. And when a woman is not pregnant, menstrual pain is perpetual—this week Mother, next week Aunt Jenny, then Alice, then her sisters as they grew older.

Why couldn't she have been a boy, she wondered. Such musing is not the much-misunderstood penis envy. A better term would be *role-in-life envy*. Alice didn't long for a penis as a possession. All she wanted was a better life.

It appeared as though the boys were having that good life. Were they really? Father was less kind to them, walloped them more. They had no place as family helpers, as farm boys do. They'd have been better off if they'd had to do the laundry, set the table, wash the dishes, help with the cooking. Those are useful skills regardless of gender. As it was, they were made to feel that they were in the way, unwanted mouths to feed. Not as close to Mother as the girls. With father there was no such thing as closeness.

So the boys were lonelier. They left home as soon as they could; they didn't feel that anyone missed them. Alice lost track of them when they were all adults. Once in a while she got a Christmas card from one of them from somewhere.

There are complex reasons why Father couldn't love the boys. He himself had come from a large family. There was too much rivalry among the brothers. He was forever testing his masculinity, was never sure of it, didn't know how to be a father to sons.

Did Father love Alice? She was his first daughter. That gave her a sort of special place. It wasn't ever said. Alice just knew it. She knew it best when his drunken tantrums extended from Mother to her. That made her feel that she mattered. It was better than being ignored. Getting what Mother got made her feel like a woman. In her fantasy, she extended the clouts in the kitchen to whatever Mother got in the bedroom as well.

When Dad became maudlin, he'd pull Alice to him, hug her, cry about life. He got her confused with his own mother, sometimes almost consciously. In the movie *Easy Rider*, one of the characters, high on acid in the days when that was the thing, hugs a statue of a woman in a cemetery. He asks, "Mother, why are you so cold?" That tells the audience how his mother was, why he was looking for love on an acid trip. It isn't any different these days. Only the fashion in drugs has changed.

That's how Alice's father's mother was. She hardly noticed her grandchildren. She was cold, critical, always quarrelling with her adult children and her children-in-law, finding fault with everyone. Alice's father married a young woman who seemed to promise more. It hardly ever works that way. Alice's mother, for her own reasons, wasn't the most understanding wife in the world. She'd had it hard as a child. Married young to get away from it. That doesn't usually work out well either.

So Dad tried to get some warmth from Alice and beer. That, too, doesn't work, except for the people who own stock in the breweries. Alice needed love, alright. But Dad wasn't giving it. He was asking for it. Alice got nothing from that except sexual stimulation, which is a bad business. She didn't know what to do with her feelings other than to feel guilty. That didn't contribute to her adult sexuality.

It's a popular misconception that people become sexually incompetent as adults because sex was treated as a taboo in their homes. Taboos are not so hard to overcome. Consider the food taboos in certain religions, for example. Many adults have little trouble giving them up and changing their food habits.

What's harder to overcome is the subtle seduction of parental need, not necessarily sexual. Alice's father was not really looking for sex with her. He was all mixed up about it. His longing for mothering mingled, as it does in every adult, with sexuality. That's because the adult body responds to physical closeness with sexual feelings. A baby takes things one step at a time. Closeness first, sexuality later. A mature adult can keep things in place, can accept sexual stirrings without acting on them in every situation.

To Alice it was terribly confusing. She needed love from her father. But what kind? Not the mixed-up kind he was able to give, which matched the mixed-up kind that any child in her position would feel. What Alice felt was normal attraction to her father. This brings us to the most subtle seduction of them all. A mature father makes his young daughter feel that she is attractive to a man. He goes about this in truly subtle ways. He admires her, buys her nice clothing if he can afford it, takes her on outings that vaguely resemble dates, embraces her but doesn't overdo. Alice's father overdid, not because he was sexually seductive, but because he was so hungry for love in the very broad sense.

The mature father, as we saw in Jane's case, seduces his daughter just enough to encourage her femininity, not so much that she thinks she stands a chance with him. The same fine line is walked by mothers with sons. Those are the optimal preconditions for a good adult love life. Parents who can walk this line convey to their children that they are attractive to the opposite sex, but that they will have to wait for a partner of the same generation.

In D. H. Lawrence's *Sons and Lovers*, the mother was unhappily married to a man she considered to be beneath her. She focused all her love, ambition, longing, loneliness, sexual frustration, wish for higher social status, upon her gifted, sensitive son. The result? He was never able to find a suitable sex partner. With a young woman who appeared appropriate, he felt he was deserting his mother. With an older woman, it felt too incestuous for comfort. His mother overstepped the line, always welcomed him too warmly when he left these women to return to her.

Alice's sexual inhibition in adulthood harks back to the time when her father overstepped this fine line in her childhood. Normally, it is the task of both parents to convey that they are married and thereby unavailable, that they are of a different generation, that children have to wait. Since her parents failed to fulfill their task, Alice had to carry theirs as well as her own.

When the parents do their jobs in this regard, the child is free to fantasize. That's what fairy tales are about. Alice could have been Cinderella or Sleeping Beauty, waiting for her prince, the man in her future, to find her. Alice was deprived of her fairy tale, so to speak. She had to become preoccupied with maintaining the incest taboo with all her might. This, then, is what creates sexual inhibition—not simply, as many people believe, because sex was prohibited by the authorities.

Alice left home soon after the two older boys did. She attended the local community college while working as a waitress. She took a business course, worked for a while as a secretary and general woman-of-all-work in a small business.

She didn't date much. John was a junior executive in her company. They started going to lunch together. But the event that led to their marriage was the office Christmas party.

Those parties usually have their share of feelers and grabbers. Some men who behave more or less like good family men and serious business men all year tend to let themselves go at the Christmas party. A few drinks and they were Alice's father all over again, except that they didn't hit her. They tried kissing that was more than too friendly, touching her if they could get away with it, dragging her into a corner.

John was the hero. He was single. Alice knew him from the few business lunches they'd had together. He took on the job of shooing the other men away at the party. He kept Alice occupied. After the party he took her home, said goodnight at the door, didn't touch her. She was his.

John's background was very different from Alice's. He was the only child of a lower-middle-class urban family. His father had a small retail business and large ambition for his son. John's father wanted him to become a lawyer or an executive in a major corporation. John went to a moderately good college and a moderately good graduate school of business. He became a middle-range executive in the small business where he met Alice. The performance did not match his father's ambition. John himself still thought he might make it bigger. In fact, he couldn't understand why this was not happening.

Very often a person fails to live up to what is expected of him because of a raging conflict with his ambitious parent. Just as often, however, it is a matter of parental overestimation of the offspring's ability. With John it was both. John's father wanted his son to be everything he, the father, was not. This left little room for what John really was and could be. He followed the path that was laid out for him. He did not follow it brilliantly because he was not all that brilliant.

John did not have it in him to rebel because he was owned by his father's ambition and his mother's need to keep him tied to her. It would have been worse for him had he tried. He would have become involved in some counterculture thing that might have been all rebellion and no accomplishment. Successful rebellion would have been wonderful for him, but one needs a bit of encouragement for that. Neither parent wanted John to venture too far from all that home represented. That was the contradiction in their message. Accomplish wonders, but don't leave us.

John's parents were first-generation Americans of immigrant parents. They had had to find their way into a world wider than the one their parents had been able to lead them into. Having left their homes, parents, siblings, everything familiar, never to return, their parents, like many immigrants once having reached these shores, were afraid to venture beyond their small ethnic neighborhood. With many exceptions, the children of these immigrants do not venture very far either. It is usually the second generation that acquires a better education and a better knowledge of the wider world.

This was John's sociological circumstance. His psychological circumstance was to have been born to a frightened mother who had lost two children before he was born and was unable to conceive again after him. He was, so to speak, the family treasure.

John was average. He was an average child whose parents

held out above-average expectations for him. They were unable to assess his abilities and limitations realistically and they were unable to relinquish ownership of him.

As an only child, he was alone with his mother almost all of his preschool years. She fussed over him. Took him to the park for fresh air even on the coldest days—bundled up of course. Forced all the right food into him. Hovered over every sneeze. When he began to toddle, she watched his every step, picked him up when he fell, worried about every bruise. She did not like it when he toddled away.

That toddlers walk away is one of the most amazing discoveries of the ego psychologists. Doesn't sound so mind blowing, does it? Anyone who looks closely can observe that. The fact is, however, that no one ever did before Margaret Mahler discovered it in the 1950s, which is rather late in human history. The Scandinavian author, Kierkegaard, describes a child running toward his mother's outstretched arms. Literary artists are usually right about such psychological matters. This one was wrong. The child's first steps are not toward, but away from.

Ego psychologists have found that the very young infant experiences herself as part of the mothering person. When the child begins to bulge out of early infancy by becoming too big to mold to the mother's body as in a cuddly carrier, the world takes on a new dimension. The child sees the person holding him from a greater distance than before. There is no longer so much body contact. The connection with mother is now maintained more by eye contact.

Watch a toddler learning how to maintain connection by means of eye contact. The beach is a good place for toddler watching. The child heads for the open sea. After some ten steps, however, he turns back to reestablish contact. Once assured that mother is still there, he marches bravely on.

That's the story of development—creating greater and greater distance, never in a straight line, always needing to be sure that home base is still there. In our culture, it takes a very long time for the child to grow up and really leave. That long march into the world away from home and mother begins at three or four months and takes twenty years or so to complete. For some, like John, it is never completed.

Technically speaking, this process is called *differentiation*. The child gradually perceives that he is a separate person, sometimes with pleasure, often with fear. Begins to take over self-ownership, acquires an identity, builds a separate life.

John's mother couldn't stand his attempts to differentiate. She tended to clutch him to her. She dressed and bathed him as though she owned his body. That's a difficult-to-discern subtle seduction. There is a way of handling a child's body as though it is your own instead of gradually affirming his ownership by turning over some of the tasks as he becomes ready. A very young child, for example, will grab the washcloth while being bathed, suck on it. At first it's a new and interesting toy. With a little help, a slightly older child quickly understands the purpose and takes over the washing job. Not as efficiently as mother, if cleanliness is overriding. Very efficiently, if encouraging the child to become himself is at least as important.

This is the moment to remind ourselves that ego psychology does not put the blame on mothers. True, John's mother, because of her own fears, could not tolerate his separateness. Some children struggle against that kind of tug a lot harder than John did. They don't always succeed if the pull is too strong. John wasn't inclined to try very hard. We don't blame him either. He simply was not that way. A tendency to opposition and rebellion can be healthy if not carried to extremes. John did not have such a tendency. It's something innate that is either there or not there. So no one was to blame. The *combination* of John as he was and his mother as she was worked out as it did.

It should also be clear by now that the situation of a mother and baby alone at home all day is a potential hot potato so far as subtle seductions are concerned. When should a child be left to bathe himself? Does he need constant supervision? Isn't it good enough to be close by to be sure that he doesn't drown? Of course he might not come out as clean, but what price cleanliness? The child's self-ownership is more important than clean ears.

This goes for girls too. In some instances it goes especially for girls. A girl's genitals must be washed delicately. They don't have to be scrubbed as though the washcloth is steel wool scrubbing a pot. Sounds strange, but some mothers forget the distinction. Scrubbing the genitals can be arousing and painful simultaneously. It gives a child an unsettling combination of sensations.

John grew up with two strikes. One was that his parents expected too much of him even before he was born. Their child, whoever he or she was, was preordained to make up for all their dashed ambition. They didn't have the education to enable them to become what they would have liked to have been. They met in the neighborhood. They fell in love and wanted to marry. In those days it was up to the man to find a way of earning a living before he could marry. John's mother wasn't trained to do anything. She wasn't expected to work after marriage. The families pitched in and helped John's father become a shopkeeper. He resigned himself to that. The children would fulfill the ambition. That's a heavy load for children to bear. As it turned out they couldn't have more than one child, so John was it.

The second strike was that John did not have outstanding ability. He was not cut out to set the world on fire. For some parents, that would be fine. He could be whatever he could be. John's parents never accepted the fact that he would be an ordinary man.

There ensued one disappointment after another as he came home from school with average grades. He was never first in his class. He never failed either. But he kept striving for more than he was capable of. This imbued him with the self-image of a failure.

Childhood social relationships were difficult for John. He could not get along in the world of children without his mother. There comes a time when a mother cannot take a child to school any longer, certainly cannot stay there with him. The separation from his mother was exceedingly painful for him because the two of them had never engaged in the gradual, mutual letting go that enables a child to become himself. He was unable to play with the other children. How could he play ball with the boys without his mother? Certainly he couldn't play with her. His father had not grown up with athletics, so it never occurred to him to play ball with John. He wouldn't have known how.

Each failure to excel made John feel more incompetent. He was living up neither to his parents expectations nor his own, which were adopted from theirs. He couldn't make friends, so he was lonely. That made him cling to his mother all the more. It became a vicious cycle. He almost couldn't function without her.

John's mother conferred with his grade-school teacher about all the small matters that children ordinarily handle by themselves. On the rare occasions when he was unable to complete his homework, she went to see the teacher with an excuse for him. Things like that did not contribute to a feeling that he could handle things on his own.

John's father didn't have much time to insert a difference. That's an important role for a father. By establishing a separate relationship with a child, he loosens the close tie that all children have, at first, with their mothers. John's father left everything up to Mother. He worked long hours in the store, seven days a week. He was far from disinterested. He was *too* interested. But he didn't know who John was, didn't understand him as a unique being. John was part of Father as well as Mother. He knew that he was expected to be everything his father wanted to be but wasn't.

When John was in high school, his mother couldn't go to see the teacher every other day. She went during open school week. Her conferences with the teachers always took longer than those with the other parents. She convinced the teachers that John was cut out to do great things in this world, and some of them gave him special consideration. This did not contribute to a feeling that he was making it on his own merit.

He did not date many girls in high school. But when he did, the relationship was very intense. He got into the girl's every move, every thought, every breath. He also got into sex and loved it. But almost more than sex, he loved talking to girls about his feelings and hers, far into the night.

It's nice for people to be able to talk about their feelings. These days, it's even a switch from times when people talked too little about their feelings. Especially now that women's feelings are acknowledged as important, men are expected to be more into talking and listening.

It can go too far. John, under the guise of being interested, sensitive, emotionally aware, was really seeking union with the other person so that they were no longer two separate people bounded by their respective skins. Each understood exactly how the other felt, what was on the other's mind. For John it was a replay of his relationship with his mother. For the girl, it was something similar out of her life experience. It never lasted. It couldn't. People who get that close reach a point at which they can't stand it any longer.

There were a few more such relationships in college and grad school. Nothing serious. Then John got a job in the company where Alice worked.

It wasn't love at first sight. It took a few years. At the Christmas party, John was simply being the good samaritan. He had been brought up that way. Married men didn't paw women. He came to her rescue.

After the party, Alice was much friendlier, which sparked John's interest. He was what some people label *passive*.

There's a good deal of confusion about what constitutes passivity. We tend to judge by action, but that can be misleading. A person who is rushing around appears to be *active*, in the ordinary sense of that word. The activity, however, may be the result of a number of factors. Take compensation, for example. A meek person may become a jock in order to conceal the meekness from self as well as others. An overanxious person may not be able to sit still. A truly active person, in the psychological sense, needn't be jumping all over the place. He may simply be a person with quiet initiative. That defines it better.

In that sense, perhaps John was passive. We have to take into account that he wasn't exceptionally talented. Maybe he was behaving appropriately, not showing off more than he could deliver. At any rate, he wouldn't have gone after Alice in a big way. She came onto him because he was made for her. That is, she had an inkling that he needed intense closeness, as did she, but that he wouldn't take her over. She was made for him too. He needed someone to take over where his mother had left off, take care of him for life, he hoped. Alice was a caretaker who didn't ask much for herself. They were tailor-made for each other.

Chapter 11

What Made Them Click

Relationships that endure, even for a short while, are held together by common needs. This says nothing new. What is not well known is that mutuality — relating, perfect understanding, being in sync, being on the same wavelength, feeling the same vibes — can get to be too much of a good thing.

Alice grew up alone in a crowd. Her inner psychological state was a paradoxical one. She both longed for and feared intense closeness. People like that are usually aware of the longing, but not of the fear. That makes them want closeness until they are on the verge of getting it. Then the unconscious fear causes them to back away.

When Alice was an infant, the time of life when intense closeness is necessary and appropriate, her mother did her duty. She nursed Alice for a few months, weaned her to a bottle as quickly as possible, held and cuddled her minimally. She wasn't a cuddling mother by temperament. Besides, she hardly had the time. So Alice had something, but it was on the short side. It made her long for more.

This builds up a stance, a mental attitude, that gets trans-posed to other relationships. One wants and denies oneself simul-taneously. This can be very confusing at those times in life when getting next to another person's skin is appropriate. The pattern of wanting and denying oneself at the same time no longer makes sense. By that time, however, it has become so ingrained that it spoils the adult relationship.

As an adult, Alice couldn't "let herself go," as the advice usu-ally has it. Over the years, she created a pattern of resisting that which she longed for. It began with having been shortchanged when she had the intense need for closeness with a mothering person that is every child's birthright. On a scale of one to ten, Alice received about five. She was more fortunate than some ba-bies who get less. Yet, it was on the short side.

There are two principal psychological times for closeness. One is in infancy, when we need the appropriate subtle seduction that acts as a psychological startup. The feeling of oneness with Mother is a sort of launching pad. Forever after, we seek that wonderful feeling of togetherness. We find something like it again in an adult relationship, one that includes the most gratify-ing kind of adult closeness—sex. The infantile experience of how good closeness feels is the template for the adult search for a part-ner with whom one can experience something resembling infan-tile togetherness *once in a while*. It can never be exactly the same, and that is why so many adult relationships are disap-pointing.

The thrust toward psychological birth severs the tie to mother. It creates ever-greater psychological distance. But it does not go in a straight line. There are pulls and tugs in both di-rections at once. The pull toward separation always has to be the greater, but there are moments when the direction is reversed. Those are the moments of pleasure, when we are reminded of that which we can never remember consciously—the times when we were cuddled infants. Those moments come when we are enjoying ourselves, having an esthetic experience, feeling intense pleasure.

When Alice was a young child, about five or so, her little sister joined her in bed. From that time on, Alice never slept by herself until she left home to go to work in another city.

There were for Alice, as there are for every child, moments of fear, distress, longing, disappointment, loneliness. Those were the moments of greatest temptation to cuddle up with someone for comfort. Fortunately for Alice, she was one of the children who knew to resist.

When Alice shared a bed with her sister it was too late for closeness, and it would have been inappropriate with a sibling. This is where the pattern of resisting served Alice so well. Later, in an adult relationship, it failed to serve her. In psychological lingo, that which had been *adaptive* became *maladaptive*. To put it in plainer language, Alice had the innate capacity to protect herself, up to a point. She did such a good job that the pattern of not yielding became fixed. She couldn't yield when, consciously, she wanted to. Advice to relax is useless in such circumstance.

Some adults describe to their therapists the lengths to which they went to get away from the sibling in the same bed. They spent their nights as children sleeping halfway off the bed, hanging over the edge!

Then there is the matter of sexuality. As we have noted, children are sexual beings without the psychological or even physical maturity for adequate discharge. Alice was aroused by her brothers in sex play during the day, by her father's drunken, irresponsible, unrestrained behavior in the evening, and by her sister at night, simply because of the body closeness. What is a child to do?

The best thing she could have done was to have found a private place where she could masturbate. This saves a child from the unbearable buildup of sexual tension and from the damage of involvement with another person. It is also a self-affirmation. Until a suitable partner is found much later in life, there is reassurance that one can give oneself pleasure independently. It is a useful step away from the closeness with Mother. It is private, secret, intact. It preserves and consolidates the self. It gives a child a breather between closeness with Mother and closeness in an adult sexual relationship.

There was no private place in Alice's home.

Is sex with another person damaging to children? We answer *yes* instinctively, especially when we are referring to the gross seductions, although few can verbalize the reason for this gut response. It might be helpful to know the reason.

The years of childhood are for self-consolidation, for self-affirmation, for finding one's boundaries. That important psychological task is impaired when it is interfered with by something as powerful as a sexual encounter. It rushes things. The timetable gets out of order.

That is the soundest non-moralistic argument against adolescent sex—not that it is wrong, bad, or even that there is the complication of possible pregnancy. The most detrimental feature is that it impairs psychological development despite the fact that, physically, the teenage child is mature enough. Psychological maturity doesn't keep pace, however, and can be halted in its tracks if something as profound as sex interferes. Premature sex can retard psychological development. If teenage sex results in parenthood, there is a double psychological impairment. The timetable again.

What is being said here is that, as children, we have to find ourselves in order that, as adults, we may lose ourselves temporarily in a sexual experience and come out of it safely.

This explains also why the gross seductions are so damaging. The child who experiences that horror not only has the violation of the generational difference to repair, but also has to overcome having been diverted from the age-appropriate task of self-consolidation. The tragedy of the gross seductions is that we are not sure that so much overcoming is possible, even with good therapy. This does not mean that therapy should not be attempted. Even where it cannot work miracles, it does some good.

Don't get upset if you slept with a sib in childhood. For an event like that to cause serious trouble, it would have to connect with approximately six other threads or, as we say in the trade, *determinants*. One of those determinants is an innate tendency for mental illness. If that is happily absent, a single experience does not break the camel's back.

The true adult is a person who has become consolidated, intact, separate from all others, with an inner life consisting of thoughts, fantasies, and even secrets that are never shared. Only an adult who meets that definition can risk the intense closeness with another person that is involved in a sexual encounter. Those who still wish to unite with another person to make up for what was missed in infancy can't make it. I have said that adult closeness only *resembles* the closeness with mother in infancy. It is not the same thing.

That might seem strange. One would think that sex is the ideal activity for gratifying the wish to unite. It is. The problem is that people like Alice and John have never become separate enough to be able to enjoy *temporary* union—Alice because she had had that taste of it and forever after wanted more, John because he had had too much and was stuck in it.

That still seems puzzling. It becomes clearer if we realize that, with such people, the unconscious longing is for a union that never ends. That's the difference between adult closeness and infantile closeness. An adult has a sense of time and, if true psychological adulthood has been attained, has completed the developmental task of childhood and adolescence—establishment of a solid and unshakable identity. It is only when that important development has not taken place that the two kinds of closeness that are really so different appear the same. Sex gets all mixed up with what was appropriate for a baby.

Where there has been too much closeness, the person has

never had the opportunity to experience gradual, tolerable separateness as well. Where there has been too little, closeness is longed for forever. This is another of those instances in which one wishes for something until it appears that it can be attained. Then there is terror lest it happen. We saw that with oedipal wishes. Now we are discussing the panic can that also come about when the wish for closeness threatens to be fulfilled. People will go to great lengths to avoid that much anxiety. They give up pleasure because survival comes first.

This accounts for many types of sexual dysfunction. The moment of orgasm involves a temporary abandonment of identity. It's the moment when we are least concerned with who we are, with our otherwise healthy self-interest, self-consciousness. We have to be very sure of ourselves to be able to give up our identity momentarily, sure we'll get it back. People like Alice and John simply cannot take that chance. They may not find themselves again.

Alice and John clicked because each felt the other's longing for closeness. They felt that they understood each other. They talked for hours about their feelings. They believed that each had to know everything about the other. There were no secrets, no silent thoughts, no unshared fantasies. It looked like an ideal marriage.

Take another look. Alice needed infantile cuddling because she had been shortchanged. John needed it because he had had so much that he never came out of it. Both lacked the intermediate developmental space that the years between infancy and adulthood ideally provide. Sex didn't work out. John was so afraid that he ejaculated before he could get in. Alice tightened up and dried up. They struggled with it but couldn't make it work. They settled for mutual masturbation once in a while.

Mostly, they avoided sex. The usual story. It was like a ballet. The choreography had them moving away from each other whenever closeness threatened. When John wanted it, Alice was tired, or had a headache, or had had a hard day with the children. On the rare occasions when Alice wanted it, John had brought work home from the office and couldn't spare the time.

Although Alice rarely wanted sex, she wanted other things. She nagged John to talk to her far into the night. They had enjoyed that early in their relationship. John began to withdraw. He wasn't into pouring out every feeling anymore. He became silent, aloof. He was trying to keep himself to himself. Belated consolidation. That never works either, because there is no end to it. The time is past. It's not like childhood, when one accomplishes a psychological task and then moves on to the next one.

So many marriages are like that. The partners get out of sync. Identity before pleasure.

Alice and John began to have fantasies that it would be better with someone else. They thought about walkouts. Some people do have extramarital affairs because the distant fields seem greener. Also, an affair involves less commitment, and therefore less fear. Alice and John couldn't bring themselves to it.

They also thought of divorce. They decided to stay together for the sake of the children. Not a bad reason.

Chapter 12

To Wrap It Up

We know a great deal about biological adaptation, about how the body adjusts to differences in climate and that sort of thing, because that was studied long before the ego psychologists studied adaptation in the psychological sense. Now that psychology has caught up with biology, we can see how infants, young children, adolescents, and even adults, use their inborn abilities to survive and adapt in both the biological and psychological realms.

But, first, what is ego psychology? Why, the psychology of the ego, of course! *Ego* is Latin for *I*. It has become a popular word in the ordinary English vocabulary, used in everyday language to refer to what ego psychologists would call *self-esteem*. It is that, and much more. Thus, we do things to enhance it, go on trips with it, feed it, boost it, and sometimes injure it or suffer its being injured by others.

The much more that the ego psychologists ascribe to the ego are our inborn abilities, plus those that we acquire as we develop. Inborn are a multitude of talents, potentials that enable the human infant to develop according to a timetable that varies only slightly from one person to another. We all have, for example, potential to sit up, crawl, walk, talk. These develop as we reach the appropriate ages. Other potentials are perception, thought, recognition, memory, intentionality, organization, and more. These are called *ego functions*.

As a science of human behavior, ego psychology is the study of human psychological development. Its foundation is psychoanalytic theory. In fact, it *is* psychoanalytic theory, brought up-to-date by the investigators who carried on Freud's work. Of special interest here are the studies of those ego psychologists who investigated child development from physical birth through the first three years of life.

Margaret S. Mahler discovered that psychological birth takes place some three years after physical birth. During those first years, we undergo the most accelerated development ever. Through Dr. Mahler's studies, combined with those of others, such as René A. Spitz, Heinz Hartmann, and Edith Jacobson, we know infinitely more about child development, and therefore about childrearing, than before.

The names of those great psychoanalytic investigators are hardly household words. They did their work quietly, published in the scientific journals, and neither sought out the media nor were sought out by them. You have not read much about them in the popular science magazines, and newspapers have not announced their discoveries in the same manner as they announce, for example, discovery of a new drug. Yet, we can no longer bring up our children without the information that they have given us.

Their guidelines teach us how to partner a child through the days, weeks, months, and years of early life in order to provide a solid foundation that will serve that person throughout later life. The psychology dictates the terminology. Parents are no longer upbringers; they are partners. That is not to say that the partnership is an equal one. Parent and child have different roles. The analogy here is to ballet. A dancer "partners" the ballerina. They have different tasks to perform, but they must dance to the same tune in the same rhythm. We speak of parental attunement.

Attunement to what? To the differing movements of the developing child. As one mother put it to me, the ego psychologists broke the code. The child's heretofore bewildering movements away from and toward the mothering person now make sense. I described this in the stories. There is a time for everything—a time to be close to mother, a time to create distance, a time for self-assertion, a time to cling. These do not arrive in an ordered sequence, and so attuned parenting is sometimes difficult. This should not be off-putting. Mistakes are as reparable as they are inevitable. If you miss one cue, you'll pick up on another. A dancer who misses a beat recovers, keeps on going, and the performance is not marred.

One of the most surprising discoveries by the ego psychologists is the nature of the inequality between child and parenting persons. We always knew that the parent-child relationship is unequal, but we used to think that it was the parent who plays the larger part. The surprise is that it is the child! This is not meant simplistically to imply that the child takes charge. It means that children, from birth on (and perhaps before), have to perform their own developmental tasks. We cannot do it for them, but we can help or hinder. My purpose has been to show how to help.

Some inborn potential does not become evident until much later than early infancy, so we cannot say that Johnny, at one month of age, is destined to become a musician, scientist, carpenter, or whatever. The abilities that count, at birth, are those that insure survival. The unique talents that are to develop in each individual can wait until the child is well along physically and psychologically.

The human infant is, in fact, rather poorly equipped for physical survival. Not only is the newborn put under a sudden strain to secure food and oxygen in an entirely new way at the moment of birth, but that has to be accomplished with still immature respiratory, digestive, and nervous systems. Compare the plight of the human infant with that of some animals who can get up on their feet shortly after birth and get themselves to the source of food. The best device the newborn human has is to cry. That is only effective if there is a mothering person to provide milk and affection, the two essentials for biological and psychological survival. An abandoned infant can announce his or her existence from the doorstep or garbage receptacle, but has to rely upon luck to be rescued. It depends altogether upon whether someone is within earshot. If the cry does not summon help, the attempt at adaptation is an attempt that fails.

But, provided there is a mothering person, the human infant has a remarkable capacity for development that goes far beyond mere survival. That is where humans are superior to the lower animals, or so we like to believe. The animals are in no position to refute us.

Another of the great discoveries of the ego psychologists, perhaps the greatest as it pertains to childrearing, is that the lion's share of adaptation rests with the infant. Human infants come into the world at a height of adaptive capacity. Therefore, parents have only to partner the development as it unfolds. Watch the cues, get to know your baby, respond in rhythm. The ego psychologists refer to this as *mutual cueing*.

The discovery that the infant plays the larger role in adaptation rescues parents from all the blameful burdens that were put on their backs by other schools of psychology. The "blank slate" school, for example, promoted the idea that parents can make of children whatever they wished. Or, you may call this same philosophy of childrearing the "lump of clay" school, which sees the child as something to be molded to one's will. Or, alternatively, you may refer to a similar idea as the "empty vessel" school of thought. Those people speak about input. They would have the child digest and metabolize whatever you choose to introduce psychologically, along with the spinach. Better still, you might call that the "child as receptacle" school.

With the ego psychological discovery about the child's innate abilities, those ideas no longer wash. Now we know that a new-born enters the world with the psychological equipment to make the adventure of development his own thing. This does not lead to chaotic, undisciplined development, however, because also in-born is a developmental timetable, or program (if you like computer language), which the developing child follows.

So, it isn't what we do *to* children that determines how they will develop. It's what they *bring* to the partnership, in combination with how attuned we are to their changing developmental needs.

To put things more technically, ego psychologists refer to infants' inborn talent for psychological adaptation as "the capacity to extract from the environment." To the newborn, the world is small indeed. The environment is usually the mothering person. She has to be there to respond, to be extracted from. This does not mean milk alone; it means psychological "supplies" as well. Those supplies have to be provided; it's up to the baby to do the extracting.

Let's take an example or two. The baby will become interested in a crib toy, have her interest awakened, will extract pleasure, entertainment, and even a form of education, from it. He will respond to your cuddling by snuggling up to you, molding to your body, cooing. Or, if you initiate babbling, the baby will engage in a "conversation" with you. You are providing the psychological supplies along with the food. That's seduction. The infant uses these seductions as developmental opportunities. That's extraction.

Everyone knows that there are lusty infants who extract from the breast with relish, and there are sluggish extractors who have to be coaxed. The same holds true for extraction of developmental supplies. Some infants are powerful extractors who can melt a heart of stone. Some are indifferent and need to be seduced. Some lack the ability to extract, no matter how much one tries to seduce.

It is this extraction that sparks interaction. It operates for life, but it is at its most effective in preparation for psychological birth. It's a long gestation. At physical birth, and for a short time thereafter, the child experiences himself as part of the mothering person. Gradually, she becomes more separate. Gradually he forms a distinct identity. That's when psychological birth takes place.

There are four possible combinations of partners:

The first consists of a child who extracts psychological supplies from the "environment" with zest, in interaction with a warm, loving, outgoing, enthusiastic parent. Obviously, that will work out exceptionally well.

The second possibility can also work out well. There, we would have a lusty extractor who has a somewhat indifferent parent. That child will "seduce" the parent into interacting.

The third possibility can also work. That is the combination of a sluggish extractor with an enthusiastic parent who "seduces" the baby into interaction.

The fourth possibility cannot work. That is the unfortunate situation in which there is an innately meager ability to extract. No matter how competent the parent, the child cannot engage in the interaction. Those are our autistic children who can function in this world to a very limited degree and have to be taken care of for life.

There is a fifth possibility, but there is no point in discussing it here. That is the sad situation of the child who is so badly abused that no amount of good endowment can overcome it. Their adult partners are too sick to benefit from reading a book.

Fashions in psychology change, sometimes for no better reason than why hemlines change. Today's fashion, which I believe is on the wane, is to be anti-Freudian. Psychotherapy, often promoted as something different from Freudian psychoanalysis, is in. Psychoanalysis is out. It is not well enough known that these two forms of treatment are not so dissimilar. For some kinds of problems, psychoanalysis is best; for others, the treatment of choice is psychotherapy. But, be sure that the choice is made by a skilled diagnostician.

And don't be fooled by the hype. Freudian theory is living and well and will survive all of the fads that proliferate around us. How do I know that psychoanalytic ego psychology is not yet another fad? Because it is not the brainstorm of one person making the statement of the moment. It is sound scientific theory based upon the investigations of many, built brick by brick, and proven in clinical trials. I have said that those theorists' names are not well known because they did not seek the limelight. Their only glory is that we know better how to help people, if we are therapists, and how to bring up our children more successfully, if we are parents.

When I am asked what I do, I say, on the days when I feel courageous, that I am a psychoanalyst. "How old-fashioned," they gasp. "Don't you know that Freud died in 1939, that he is passé?" "Yes," I reply. "And do you know when Sir Isaac Newton died?" No one remembers that date, but they do know that the science of physics is flourishing, thanks to fact that Newton's successors built upon his discoveries rather than having discarded them in favor of the fad of the week. Freud's successors have continued where he left off, in the same fashion as in any science. Somehow, the detractors, who would discover the wheel all over again, get a better press.

If, instead of announcing that I'm a psychoanalyst, I were to soft peddle and say that I'm a psychotherapist, there would be nods of approval. But then, if I were to add that I am a psychoanalytically oriented psychotherapist, the gasping would begin all over again. And, if I were to say that I'm an ego psychological, psychoanalytically oriented psychotherapist, I'd lose my audience.

Approximately fifty years ago, a psychologist named Watson proposed a theory that he called *behaviorism*. That is not the same as the behavior modification that is practiced today. It was the granddaddy of modern behavior mod.

Watson was a "molder." He believed that one can train a child to become whatever the trainer desired. His ideas had a far-reaching effect upon education and childrearing. He advocated, among other things, feeding infants on a strict four-hour schedule, and not picking them up in between. What happened to those babies?

There are many fifty year olds walking around today who are in their right minds despite having been fed on a strict schedule. It takes more than that to do extreme damage. They didn't get away scot-free, however. Imagine the pain experienced by a baby with a tiny stomach who gets hungry after three hours and has to wait an hour, not even being picked up and comforted during the ordeal! That's a terrible introduction to life.

It sets a pattern. Life is painful. Pain has to be endured. Comfort is hard to come by. The "Watsonian babies" I have seen as adults are enured to suffering. They find life harder than it needs to be. They also lack maximum ability to relate to others because, as babies, they had to find comfort within themselves. Bobby was one of those babies, even though he is younger than those brought up by Watson's regime. We saw how he turned inward, not from a single cause, but from a series of experiences.

Many present-day fifty year olds escaped. They were the lucky ones who had "good enough" parents who couldn't bear to follow Watson's instructions. Many parents of fifty years ago picked up their babies to ease their pain. They fed them when they were hungry, not when Watson said they should. They paid the price of feeling guilty for being good parents.

People who are confident enough to know that they don't look good in the latest designer clothes don't wear them. They'd rather look out of style than wear something unbecoming. Parents who are confident about their own good sense don't follow every childrearing fad.

After a while, the fashion changed. Watsonian behaviorism went out and the backlash, overpermissiveness, came in. Then, the advice was to yield to the child's every whim. Children were permitted to rule the family as though they had ultimate wisdom. They decided when to eat, when to sleep, when to play. Worst of all, they owned the adults who catered to them. They were a confused and worried generation. The parents were not in charge. The kids felt lost. No matter how well provided for physically, they were neglected children.

We see this still, no longer because the parents are following some mistaken guidebook. Some parents are unable to take charge. Trouble sometimes doesn't show up until their kids are teenagers because that's when they are big enough to get around on their own and make big trouble. It only gets harder with the passage of time. Because they weren't disciplined before, one now has to discipline a child who has the body of an adult and the arguments of a Philadelphia lawyer.

One of the important lessons of these swings in fashion is that we appreciate the value of the generation gap. To repeat, child and parent are partners, but not equal ones. Children are no longer required to make decisions and to take charge of situations that are beyond their wisdom, knowledge, experience, and psychological readiness. They are relieved that the adults know what to do without consulting them. That doesn't mean that we don't listen to children. We listen more closely than ever. It means that adults take the responsibility for exercising judgment that children, in their inexperience, don't possess. The role of the older generation is to provide structure, rules to live by, reliability, leadership, judgment. When we do that, children feel secure.

Ego psychology tells us what is appropriate at every stage of development. A very young infant is not spoiled by being made comfortable, as Watson mistakenly thought. Good feelings in infancy set the person's outlook on life. There are many terms for this—confident expectation, optimism, self-esteem. Lucky people have it because they have been "seduced" into feeling good from the start. Egos that have had such a good startup do not have to be continuously boosted in adult life. We all need an ego boost once in a while, though. No one ever becomes so complete unto himself that he can get along without a brief ego trip. That's different from Bob, who needed it all the time.

As children get older, they also have to be frustrated at times.

The "overpermissiveness" people did not understand the importance of frustration for development. Frustration is essential at the right time, in the right dosage. We cannot, without penalty, frustrate for its own sake to gratify our mean streaks. But children need small doses of "good" frustration to get used to the fact that they cannot have everything they want.

It has to be reasonable, however. Children know when parents are being unfair. Ego psychologists use the phrase *optimal frustration*. It means, not so much that the child suffers unnecessarily, not so little that no psychological growth takes place.

Some things appear arbitrary. Do it anyway. Children have to go to bed at a reasonable hour. They can live without a cookie before lunch, despite the anguished screams. They have to learn to be alone in order to be able to entertain themselves, not only with their toys, or tape recorders, or TV, but also with their fantasies, their inner thoughts. Being quietly alone helps people think. Tell that to your taxi driver.

They also have to learn, not too soon, but not too late either, that other people have needs. I once heard a five year old exclaim, as though making a new discovery, "Mommies have to eat too." Five years is too late to come to that realization. One can imagine that that mother had been so much at her child's beck and call that she never took a moment for herself.

Frustration has not only to be reasonable, but it must also be imposed at the phase appropriate time. Translate that to mean that an older child can tolerate a bit more frustration than a baby can. Frustration can promote development *if* it is not cruel, *if* it is not too much, and *especially if* the gratifications counterbalance it.

How can frustration help a child grow? I am not referring to the deliberately mean kinds of things that some sadists impose to make a child suffer. Children can only grow backward from those. I mean something else. Maybe you wouldn't even call it frustration.

I have described it in my emphasis on the value of aloneness, space to grow, to establish boundaries. By that definition, going to bed alone is a frustration that helps a child grow. Even in early infancy, when cuddling is as essential as food, the baby needs time to be alone. As I showed in the stories, that's how the boundaries of one's body are established. The baby lies in the crib, explores his body, sucks her toes, discovers his genitals. This is *I*. The child learns to speak, begins to use the first-person pronoun. An ego is born.

Then it can be said that the person has a *mental representation,* an image in the mind, of her body. It is called the *body ego.* We are not born with it. It needs time and space to develop. When we have it down pat, which takes many years, one adult can be in bed with another without danger to development, to identity. Spending eight hours or more out of every twenty-four next to another body in childhood impairs development while it is still in progress. That also holds for adolescence. Don't be deceived by the physical development. An adolescent is still a developing child, psychologically. Don't treat him as you would a *young* child, but don't treat him as an adult either.

We have come full circle in two generations. Watson imposed too much frustration. The "overpermissive" people bent over backward in the opposite direction. They practiced overindulgence, which failed to prepare their children for the realities of life. Now we hope we have achieved a happy balance. The ego psychologists have studied development in such fine detail that they know the "whens" and "how muches" – when to gratify, when to seduce, when to frustrate, how much is enough, how much is too much.

That's what they mean by *phase-specific* or *age-appropriate.* What is appropriate for psychological development at one time is out of phase at another. The young infant needs closeness. The toddler needs freedom to roam. The one and a half year old, who has roamed a bit, needs to return to home base and cling for a while before setting forth again.

Perhaps the most difficult-to-accept idea that I have introduced is that we have unconscious fantasies. Maybe it is so difficult because we don't like to think that our behavior is dictated by forces outside our control, that not all that we do is done out of free will. I have demonstrated the role of unconscious fantasy in psychological life, how it begins with a simple fantasy and builds as experience makes the individual more and more sophisticated. Little Billy started with easily understood childhood fantasies and ended with very complex ones. Finally, he had no idea what drove him to the videos. There were so many threads that he needed a skilled psychoanalyst to help him unravel them.

I also showed that there is unconscious communication. Billy's mother didn't know that she was squeamish about handling a boy baby, but it got across to him without ever being said in so many words.

Don't discard these ideas even if you don't like them. Try living with them because they're living with you. As you come to understand them, you may understand some of your otherwise inexplicable behavior. Have you ever mistaken a stranger for someone familiar? Think of it as wishing to see the familiar person. You can teach yourself to understand your unconscious in that way.

Better still, read Freud's *Psychopathology of Everyday Life*. It's one of his easier-to-understand pieces of writing. I'm convinced that you'll be convinced that we forget names, misplace things, act in otherwise perplexing ways because unconscious fantasies are at work all of the time.

You may even become convinced that we'd be empty inside without them. Life would be drab and colorless. That does happen. Some people have an impoverished fantasy life. That is the plight of people who are constantly seeking some new excitement. On the other hand, some people have too rich a fantasy life. It has to be in balance with a solid respect for reality, lest life be lived as though it's a fairy tale.

Perhaps the most inconvenient-to-carry-out idea that I have

introduced is that separation from the mothering person for prolonged periods of time is difficult for a child before psychological birth. That is not the time to take long vacations or even to send the child to visit Grandma. Wait a while. An older child can tolerate it without pain.

And, in addition to the pain when it happens, premature toolong separation renders the person prone to separation anxiety for life. How can we weigh and measure? It has been done for us. A newborn has to get used to a few familiar persons, so don't change them around. When you have become meaningful to the child, don't leave for more than a few hours at a time. As the child acquires *mental representations*, they will be used to keep your image alive in the child's mind. Then you can leave for longer periods.

Above all, remember accumulation. It will not matter a great deal if you go away and return, unless the separation is reinforced by later experience. Sometimes a parent has to go away, to a hospital, for example. Why go when it isn't necessary? You don't know what the future will bring. I have shown how trauma accumulates like compound interest. If you don't impose unnecessary trauma, the necessary ones will have nothing with which to connect.

It doesn't mean that you cannot go on vacation. It seems strange to have to say it, but many years in practice have taught me that some people think of vacation as vacation from young children. Sure, we'd all like to get away sometimes. But I said at the outset that parenting is living. There is no vacation from parenthood because there is no vacation from life. Even when your children are older and can go to camp, Grandma, school, college, they need you to be where they can locate you on a map.

Very young children don't know geography. Worse still, they do not yet have the ability to know that you will return. They are anguished to think that you have disappeared from the face of the earth. Then, when you do come back, they give you the cold shoulder to show you how it feels. Don't take it as retaliation. Children do not have words for their feelings, so they express them by demonstration.

Perhaps the most controversial idea I have introduced is that divorce is too devastating to children to be undertaken without heavy consideration for them, even if the marriage was not made in heaven for you. Heaven can wait, in many instances. There are, of course, conditions under which divorce is appropriate, such as where one spouse is damaging the other and the children. Short of that, think hard before you act.

There are whole flocks of children these days who are moved around, displaced by divorce and remarriage. That was Bob's situation. Many children are living not very great lives with a single parent. Others are shuttled from one parent to another because of divorce. Many of those marriages could have been repaired without quick resort to divorce.

Perhaps another against-the-tide matter is about custody, especially joint custody. Whoever came up with that idea was not thinking of children. It is an adult way of slicing the pie. Children need to have *one* home, their own space. More than one confuses them, as we saw with Bobby. Don't ask whether they like the arrangements you have made. They'll tell you that they love living in two places. That's what you want to hear, isn't it?

Children of divorce believe that it is their fault. They don't want to make more trouble by asserting their rights. We hear a lot about the rights of fathers these days because mostly mothers get custody. The rights of children take precedence over the rights of fathers (or mothers). That does not disregard that it is painful to have less access to the children than one might enjoy. But the children in their developmental years have the overriding right to optimal developmental opportunity, however that may be arranged.

And if you have accepted what I have had to say about fantasies, you will realize that life after divorce is hardly ever as rosy as one imagines it will be. The grass isn't greener. Miss or Mister

Right isn't out there waiting for you. If you haven't worked hard enough on one relationship, chances are that you won't do better the next time. A relationship has to be worked on for the duration. Many relationships founder because too much is expected of them. The next one won't be Paradise either. And marriage is not designed to make up for expulsion from the Garden of Eden. It was the reason for expulsion in the first place!

The story of Genesis is a beautiful metaphor, which the creation "scientists" would destroy by their concrete thinking. As a metaphor, it represents the time when life was experienced as perfect. Paradise means being competently partnered in infancy. Paradise is lost when we discover that life has its imperfections.

There are compensations. The wider world is more interesting. And there is sex out there.

Perhaps the most against-the-tide matter that I have to introduce here is that marriage counseling, by the method of seeing a couple together, has limited value. I am aware that this goes against the prevailing fad of "couple therapy." I do not treat the "marriage" or the "relationship" because I do not believe such entities exist. There are two distinct *individuals* in a relationship. I treat the individual, the problems, demands, needs, inappropriate expectations, that he or she brings to the relationship. If those can be cleared away the relationship improves.

Alice and John, for example, could not have been treated by so-called couple therapy because, although they were out of sync, the causes for each were different. In fact, they were opposite. Alice had had too little closeness, John too much. Therapy for each of these would have had to pursue different courses.

Another against-the-tide matter is that sex therapy has serious limitations. Sex is not as simple as it should be because of the complex psychological development that the human animal has to undergo. Many psychological problems take their tolls in sexual problems. Sex therapists have a new term, *sexual dysfunction*. That covers a multitude of problems that are more accurately designated as *symptoms*. The term *symptom* implies that there is something complex underneath, while *dysfunction* suggests that it can be fixed superficially. If your car has a dysfunction, you take it to a mechanic. He tunes up the ignition and your car starts again.

Sex therapy is mechanical if it treats symptoms to the exclusion of causes. A few sex problems can be "fixed" mechanically. Most of these fixes cannot last, and gimmicks do not help the more severe sexual problems, even in the short run. I have had several patients with serious sex problems caused by problems in relating. Some of them tried sex therapy to no avail. Alice, for example, could not have benefited from sex therapy because, for her, letting go meant letting go of her life, her identity. The French, reputed to be experts in sexual matters, know the difference between "the little death" and the real thing. Alice couldn't tell the difference, and she was not ready for the big one.

The mechanical gimmicks are analogous to treating a headache with aspirin. We all do that, and it helps many a headache. Sometimes, however, brain surgery is the only way. In my own practice I do both. I try to get the mechanical problem out of the way so that we can go deeper. Sometimes it will not get out of the way. It remains until the underlying causes are cleared away.

Perhaps another controversial thing I have said is that partnered sex is for adults. Everyone agrees with that in relation to young children. Where we get lost is in failure to realize that teenagers are still children. Many people are confused about teenage sex. They feel vaguely uneasy about it. Because they are big enough, are they really old enough? The reasoning of the moralists is not persuasive to many, but then they don't know what else to think. I hope I have inserted something worth thinking about— that teenagers are physically, but not psychologically, equipped for sex with another person because identity is not yet fully established.

I had the experience of teaching two different groups of university students. The undergraduates, at the upper end of adolescence, were incensed when I said that sex is for adults. The graduate students, some in their thirties and forties, agreed heartily when I said that adolescents can wait.

Perhaps not so controversial is that children should not have to be called upon to provide emotional supplies. They do it when it serves their development. Consideration for the feelings of others is an important matter for the developing child to learn. That doesn't mean that children can be used to fill in the gaps in our own emotional needs.

We all have them. Unfulfilled emotional needs exist in the best of us. No one is so perfectly fulfilled that she or he doesn't feel lonely, unloved, misunderstood, depressed, needy, at times. We have to keep it to ourselves, or get comfort elsewhere, from another adult maybe. Even there, in a marriage or similar relationship, the partner cannot be expected to fill all the gaps.

A child is overtaxed when demands clash with developmental needs. If you are lonely and the child needs space to grow, the child is crowded if you intrude. Children tend to try to meet those demands, but that distorts childhood. Many a patient has said to me that the roles became reversed, that the child had to parent the parents. In extreme form, that is the lot of children of alcoholics and drug addicts. In milder form, it happens in every family to some degree. All we can do is keep it to a minimum.

That doesn't mean that there are no rewards to be had from children. Children will give a lot spontaneously when *they* need to be loving, to return some of what we have given them. It's good for them to do that, to become able to reciprocate. They are more likely to do it when they feel it, not necessarily when it is demanded.

Then you can be sure that, when they feel it, it meets the developmental need of the moment. When your child offers you a lick of the ice cream cone, a great moment has arrived. The child wants to give you pleasure, wants you to enjoy it as he or she does. Developmentally speaking, the child has taken a huge step toward the realization that another person has needs, feelings. Not the least of it is that a more altruistic form of love is developing. Do you know some adults who haven't come that far?

My main theme, of course, has been that seduction isn't all bad. In the sense in which I have used that word, seduction is what makes life interesting. The discovery about adaptation and about the inborn capacity to adapt, to extract, to engage in interaction, says that we are born seducers. For the child, it is a life-saver, an instrument for survival. The well-endowed child uses it for those purposes. The adult partner seduces to stimulate, encourage, support, interact *and enjoy* the child's developmental progress.

When seduction goes wild it can cause big trouble. This book has been about the uses of tamed seduction.

Index